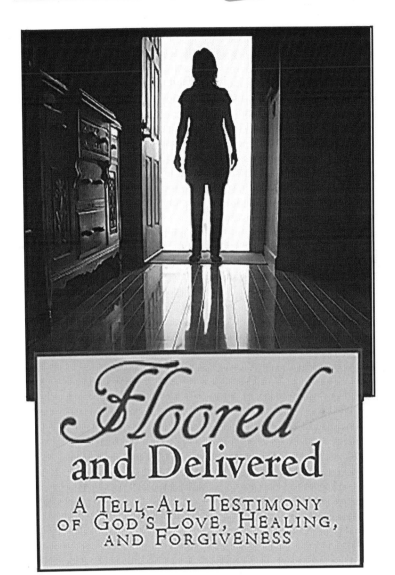

Floored
and Delivered

A Tell-All Testimony of God's Love, Healing, and Forgiveness

With Love & Truth

Elizabeth Soldahl

Elizabeth

Cover Photo and Design by: Grayson Soldahl
Interior Design by Courtney Bowers Artiste

The cover photo of this book is of Elizabeth, standing in the front doorway of her home. The reflection on the hardwood floor is where she lay lifeless the night when she was "Floored."

Order Books on Amazon.com

Contact information:
elizabethsoldahl@yahoo.com
Website: www.faithonfire.net

—Sprawled on the hardwood kitchen floor at 3 a.m., I clutched my stomach. The pain in my gut was like a knife. Feebly I called to my husband upstairs, "Honey, I need you!" Then everything went black—

What Readers are Saying:

"A compelling story! Elizabeth dares to tell about her dramatic past in truth and love. If you've suffered from sexual abuse, divorce or medical issues, read this book!" Mary E. Logan

"Loved it! A life transforming book. I could not put it down. I plan to read it again this summer, only next time more slowly." Sue S.

"Elizabeth is incredibly honest and speaks from deep in her heart. God bless you Elizabeth for sharing your story!" Karen Jones

"Her story is powerful, chaotic, addictive and reassuring." Dr. Mark

"This testimony made me cry and laugh out loud. I couldn't put it down." Billie B.

"Elizabeth's story resonated with my story. Her testimony will stir you." Kats B.

"The author's ups and downs are woven beautifully and seamlessly throughout. I also enjoyed the helpful tips at the back of the book." Deborah D.

Preface

We are all born with God-given gifts. I believe my God given gifts are encouraging others and revealing the truth. Telling the truth has often caused me trouble.

Nevertheless, my deepest nature always beckons; the longing for honesty, transparency, joy and truth. In that spirit, I reveal my life; the blessings and sorrows, the sunny days and dark storms.

My greatest desire in presenting this story is to encourage others on their journey and inspire them to never give up. Throughout my life, the ultimate Truth has set me free. I hope it sets you free too.

Jesus love, Elizabeth

"All things work together for good to those who love God..."
(Romans 8:28)

Dedication

My life is dedicated to God for His constant love, healing and forgiveness. By His grace I was delivered into freedom.

My story is dedicated to my handsome and devoted husband, Eric Soldahl. He swept me up onto the white horse and held me close through all my trials. I hang on tightly as we gallop boldly on this daring adventure.

"Be strong and of good courage. Do not be afraid or dismayed; for the One with us is greater than the one with the king...with him is an army of flesh, but with us is the Lord our God!"
(2 Chronicles 32:7-8 *Paraphrased*)

~Born as "Betsy"~

Life began with everyone calling me "Betsy," even though my God-given name at birth was Elizabeth. I grew up in sunny Santa Barbara with conscientious parents, two older Eagle Scout brothers and a scruffy dog named Turk. As a toddler, I helped Mom in the kitchen, played dolls with my friends, and wrestled with my big brothers. Sometimes in the mud. Back then, almost everyone in Southern California attended Church on Sunday. The stores were closed too. Each summer our family of five visited Lake Michigan and stayed at our Grandparents log cabin lake home for a few weeks.

Covered in mud —Brother Mark says, "Betsy is in trouble!"

~Corn on the Cob and Canoes~

The Michigan summers seemed endless, yet I longed to be home with my little friends in our safe and sleepy ocean side town. Even so, adventures were limitless at North Lake Leelanau in the middle of Michigan. It was the land of lush trees, deep lakes, wild blackberries, corn on the cob, canoeing, mosquitoes, and fireflies that lit up our games at night.

We stayed at Gramps' and Grandmother's musty old log cabin right on the Lake. It was a short drive from Ann Arbor, where they had a palatial brick home with seven fireplaces. I could not even count all the bedrooms.

There was swimming and canoeing with my older brothers, Don and Mark, and our three cousins. We loved the half mile wide North Lake, which the log cabin overlooked. Sometimes the older kids would get us to sneak out at night to skinny dip in the crisp Michigan waters. White butts flashed at the moon as we swam along like minnows and dove toward the sludgy bottom of the lake. I was usually the youngest of the group and always tried to keep up with the older kids; staying up late and rising at dawn.

"Let's swim across the lake!" my brothers would say.

I was the first in my Speedo swimsuit, treading water next to the canoe. It was the summer before kindergarten. Manning the canoe was my Dad or my Gramps. They would follow us across the lake to keep us safe.

"Keep your head above water so you don't get run over by a speedboat," Dad said.

I would swim fast to keep up with the group. The lake was cold. It seemed to take hours crossing the lake. The smallest of all, I usually made it to the other shore without any assistance from the canoe escort.

One of my favorite things was when my brothers would tip the canoe upside-down in the middle of the lake, trapping air inside of it. It was like a little bubble-cave, and we would gather under the canoe and sing, talk and tell scary stories about the lake. My voice would echo even when I whispered secrets to my cousins.

Sometimes my brothers would challenge me to swim to the bottom of the thirty foot deep lake. I usually accepted the challenge. Plunging into the snow melted water; I would swim deeper and deeper. The water became colder and colder the farther I dove. I could not see the bottom of the lake as it was so murky. My lungs would run out of air, and it seemed like I would never reach the bottom.

Swim Betsy swim, I thought to myself underwater. My lungs deflated like a balloon after turning around and my toes would often touch a rock or the sludgy bottom of North Lake. It felt like I might get stuck there. Instinctively, I would bolt up toward the sunshine like a speedy guppy. Popping through the glassy lake surface, I would proudly screech,

"I touched the bottom of the lake!"

In the evenings, all of us Logan cousins would brag over our accomplishments, as we gobbled down ketchup covered hamburgers, on the screened-in porch. There was nothing better than fresh picked corn-on-the cob drenched in butter. The cottage by the lake filled up with grandparents, Mom and Dad, siblings, aunts, uncles and cousins. I always got extra "kudos" for being so little, yet so brave and strong.

"Betsy, how do you keep up with all of those older brothers and cousins?" my dad asked.

In hot or cold water, I would often need to encourage myself to *"Swim Betsy Swim."*

~Swim Competition~

That fall back home in our Santa Barbara beach town,

I was swimming every day. Mom and Dad had signed me up to be on the La Cumbre swim team.

Early one Saturday morning, I was frozen in position on a wooden starting block. I was barely three feet tall. With arms back and knees bent, I gazed at the Olympic sized swimming pool at UC Santa Barbara. The water seemed far away.

Over the loudspeaker came a booming voice: "On your mark – get set..."

"Bang!" The starter gun sounded, and I felt a tap on my butt. My toes pressed off the edge of the cube and my body slid fingers first into the ice cold water. Once again I swam frantically for my life. I was afraid of losing. It was a big scary pool and I wanted to get out as soon as possible; so I swam.

As I stretched my hand to the far side of the pool, I touched the edge and flip-turned. Now I was on the home stretch. My tight bathing cap and the icy splashing water slightly muffled the cheering voices; however the screaming noise caused my adrenaline to pump even more. As I slapped the finish wall, I jumped out of the pool and grabbed the towel my dad had waiting for me and ran to a corner wrapped up completely with the terry cloth.

Later that morning, the results were revealed; I had won the race! Maybe I swam the fastest, not only out of fear, but also to please my parents. Then I found out Mom had tapped my bottom on the starting block because I was so paralyzed from the start.

I preferred playing with my dog and friends over swim competitions. I loved packing picnics and camping with the family. Our family traveled back to Michigan every summer for a month to see the relatives and celebrate the Fourth of July.

~Gramps~

In the midst of my All-American upbringing, there was a dark secret. From earliest childhood, I remember Gramps reading to me during my afternoon naptime. He would read me his favorite book, *"Epaminondas."* It was a racist book about a little black boy who did things that were wrong. He would step in freshly baked pies or worse. Gramps would do things to me during naptime that he should not have been doing either. His favorite line in the book would come with a big chuckle, *"Epaminondas, you ain't got the sense you was born with!"* Going forward in my life, I would discover that people with different color skin than mine often had the *best* advice; or greatest wisdom and common sense. Just the opposite of what that book implied. Maybe it was Gramps that lacked sense.

*****

One day, I peered down the old musty wooden stairs and saw the back of my Gramps' white haired head as he was standing in front of the rusty white refrigerator in the basement. My five-year-old breath was quiet as could be. My tiny fingers pressed down on my daisy flowered cotton dress as I saw the pink bottle of Lancer's Wine above his head. He drank straight out of the bottle. The back of my sneakers slowly edged up the stairs as I slipped back into the kitchen of the North Lake log cabin.

I liked my Gramps. He called me "Cookie," told funny jokes, baked bread, and had often taken me and my brothers canoeing. He was a dentist in Ann Arbor Michigan and was almost elected mayor of the town. But then there was his secret. The adults around him may have known something was amiss, but no one would dare say a thing. My grandfather was revered within the family and community.

Gramps began a pattern of fondling me when no one was looking. He had thick fat fingers with black dry cracks that wandered under my favorite floral dress and into my cotton panties during naptime. I held the book steadily as he read, not realizing then how wrong it all was.

The summer I turned six years old, I told my parents about Gramps. I skipped the details of the piggy back rides, where his thumbs slipped past the elastic of my underwear to rub my private parts as he walked around the house. I simply said,

"Gramps touches me where I go pee-pee,"

My mother seemed very alarmed.

Mom said, "Oh no, that's terrible!"

As a kindergartner, I didn't know it was wrong. After Mom's strong reaction, and being the little pleaser that I was, I slinked out of the room, afraid I had caused a big ordeal. My revealing the truth would often cause alarm in others. There was never any other mention of my naps with him. I napped alone after that summer. Mom and Dad kept him away from me at naptime. My grandfather no longer called me 'Cookie.' At some level, he must have known that I had told my mom the truth.

Soon after, he began teasing me. One time when I squinted from the bright sunlight, Gramps said, "How can you see out of just one eye?" He would contort his face and close one eye making fun of me in front of my brothers and cousins.

After our month in Michigan, we returned to the West Coast where Girl Scouts, swimming and baton competitions would keep me moving forward. I was from a family of "high achievers."

~The Light Blue Pill~

The next spring, Grandma Eckert, my mom's mom, came to visit us in Santa Barbara. Mom and Dad were going to a Medical

Conference for my Dad's work, as he was a doctor at the local clinic. Grandma would be taking care of me and my two brothers.

Before leaving, I overheard Dad telling Grandma, "If Betsy doesn't have a bowel movement for another day or so, you need to use this."

Maybe I needed to pay more attention to their conversation. There would be trouble ahead. I was always distracted playing games or "house" in the tree fort with my friends.

Apparently a couple of days passed without me going *number two*. On a bright Saturday morning, Grandma came in to the kitchen with a *HUGE* light blue pill in her hand, the size of a home-grown chubby two inch carrot.

Grandma said, "Bets, I need to use this pill."

"What?" I chirped nervously.

Grandma told me she needed to put it in my bottom since I hadn't had a bowel movement.

"What?!" I shrieked louder and started to run away.

I screamed, "Noooo!"

Then I ran as fast as my two little legs would go; through the kitchen and into the living room. I looped around and around in a circle. Grandma was chasing me saying, "Stop, Bets—Stop!"

There was no way in heck I was going to stop and have her put that *huge Horse Pill* in my butt. I ran and ran as my brothers jumped up and down cheering me on:

"Go Bets...Go!!!"

I looped around one time, two times, and on the third loop as I skidded into the kitchen, Grandma was standing right in front of me with her legs wide and her arms in a "T." Gram had tricked me. She had stopped chasing me and waited to catch me. Then she grabbed me and dutifully pinned me down on the floor. As she forced the blue horse pill between my tight white butt-cheeks, I screamed bloody murder. I was no match for her. Grandma was strong and German. Grandma and the light blue pill won.

Afterwards, I cried as I ran off to my bedroom. I locked the door and sulked for the rest of the day. Maybe I pooped later that day. I don't remember. I still loved my Grandma, but things were never quite the same between us. First Gramps, and now Grandma, with the horse pill, had touched me below the waist.

~Dentures~

It was hard for me to pack for the summer trips to Michigan. I wonder if part of my reluctance to go was because I was afraid to be alone with Gramps.

It was my job in the family to keep everyone happy and not cause any problems. There was a subtle message to "keep things to myself." So I packed slowly, and boarded the friendly skies of United Airlines along with my family.

"Hurry up, Bets!" Dad would say while we loaded the car for the airport.

Arriving back in Michigan, the summer days were long, lazy and humid. I looked forward to rolling down the Sleeping Bear Sand Dunes, along the national lakeshore. The dunes were four hundred and fifty feet above Lake Michigan. We barreled down the steep sandy side of the dunes like a rolling pin.

Back at the cabin though, there was always the looming threat of Gramps and what he might do next. Grandma Eckert lived alone as a widow in Lansing Michigan. She frequently visited North Lake sharing my little wood cabin room upstairs. I was her only granddaughter, so she spoiled me. There were little girl gifts such as combs, jewelry boxes and rings.

Often we would canoe together and look for the famous blue heron's nest in the brush. Sometimes we would bake zucchini or banana bread together. One of my favorite activities was helping her clean her "teeth." When she took out her teeth at night, I would beg her to let me shake the white cleaning powder on her dentures before dropping them in the glass of water.

In the morning I would wake up early with Gram. She was always in her own bed. I often slept on a rollaway nearby.

"Grandma, can I shake some powder on your teeth?" I begged. I held up the clear glass with her dentures next to the bed.

"Let's go find a sink so it doesn't make a mess," Grandma would say, reluctantly letting me help her. The morning powder helped "glue the teeth," inside the mouth, she explained.

Careful and nimble I was there to help. Grandma would pop the teeth into her mouth and off we would go on our day. *She had a nice smile*, I thought, as we headed off to canoe or drive to town on errands. Soon it would be nighttime, and I would be shaking the cleaning powder once again. I forgot all about the blue pill.

Saying goodbye that summer, I said, "I'm going to be in a big parade twirling my baton when we get home, Grandma!"

Baton Twirling in Santa Barbara Parade

~Tree Swing~

One summer, Gramps built a tree swing, and it swept out over the lake making it exhilarating and scary all at once. I would climb up the side of the huge tree trunk on two by four boards on a ladder of sorts. Once to the wood board platform, super high up, at the big "V" in the tree, the excitement began. A buddy would climb part way up the ladder and hand the swing to me at the landing pad. The swing only had one huge rope that threaded through a hole in the middle of the wood seat and had a knot underneath to hold it on. The rope attached to a thick branch way up high. Next, I would put the rope between my legs, sit securely on the wood swing, hang on tight, and take a deep breath. It was as if the lake was glistening with silver smiley faces at me, as my brothers cheered me on.

"Jump! Jump to the right, Bets! Jump!"

My sunburned body swung out to the right, over the lake in a circular motion. My heart was racing and my face was frozen in fear and delight as I flew through the air. Life was a daring adventure, and I was alive! It was a bit tricky, because as the full circle completed, I had to push off the tree with my feet or hands to keep from crashing into it. Then I would swing around a few more times as the circles got smaller.

That summer I learned my "right" from my "left." Even today, when in a moment of confusion, when I can't remember my right from my left, I look at my right hand and hear the echo in my ear, "Jump to the right, Bets! Jump to the right!" Having two older brothers, I was learning to take risks in my life.

Tree Swing over North Lake in Michigan

~Sleep-overs and Sunday school~

As a little girl, I had my own bedroom. I felt so lonely at night. My brothers shared a room together and my parents had each other. Sometimes I was afraid in my room and hid under the covers.

"I'm the only one sleeping by myself in the family," I said at breakfast one morning. "It's not fair!"

Most mornings I climbed into bed with my parents. "Can I have a baby sister?" I asked. "Please?" With my index finger, I drew imaginary pictures on their faces. I always wanted to make my parents happy.

The night-time loneliness went away when there were sleep-overs with my friends: Esther, Keven and Amy.

On these Saturday night sleep-overs, we would attend each other's church the next morning for Sunday School.

Staying over at Esther's, we were always busy baking cookies, twirling batons and playing with our dogs. We talked about cute boys in school as we got older.

Esther's mom would have us get up early in the morning and read our Bibles in bed. We would read about David and Goliath and Daniel in the Lion's Den. They were all so brave. When we read about Joseph in his coat of many colors, I thought he sounded like a prince. Maybe I would find a prince charming someday. But for now I desired a sister and best friends.

I learned in Sunday School in Santa Barbara that Jesus would always be my "best friend." But I still begged my parents to have a baby sister, so that I would have a best friend in my bedroom too.

~Dodge Ball~

I liked to play Dodge Ball at my elementary school in Santa Barbara. In second grade I was the smallest and youngest in my class and fast on my feet. Having two older brothers at home made me scrappy and feisty. One hot recess on the asphalt court, I found God was real.

*****

Sweat dripped down my pink cheeks as my little navy lace-up Keds sneakers darted around the gravely basketball court. I was one of the last three people running around the court, who was safe from being hit. The strong sixth grade boys threw the ball so hard and fast to try to hit me with the ball and get me "out." Once again I raced as if my life depended on it, dodging and darting the hard, white volley-ball.

"Oh, God help me!" I panted softly as the ball whizzed behind my arched back. There were a few cute boys that I wanted to impress, and I just didn't want to get hit or be "out."

It was down to just two of us on the court, and by now, I was scared. My legs were rubbery as I breathed to God again,

"Please God; help me dodge this ball..."

I wanted to believe God would help me as I raced around. In fact, one Sunday I had said a little prayer and accepted Jesus into my heart.

The ball whizzed over my head, as I hunched over and slammed on the brakes. "Wham!" the only other kid left on the court was hit squarely in the back and was eliminated. I was the last one left standing on the court! Glancing around, I wondered what to do next. Then everyone cheered as the recess bell rang. Still scared, but also thrilled, I ran all the way back to the classroom.

I sat at my little desk panting and whispered, "Thank you God."

A tear slipped out of one eye and dropped on my dress, right over my heart. I rubbed it onto my flowered outfit.

When I looked up Mrs. Fisher announced, "Ok class it's time to work on your reading folders, please get your work out of the boxes and work alone quietly."

My heart was still pumping fast.

On that day on the dodge ball court, God became my friend. He saved me. And as my life unfolded, He would save me again and again and again. But for now I would learn to stay quiet and keep dodging what life threw my way.

~Losing my Voice~

I became rather shy throughout elementary and middle school. I thought; *maybe no one wants to hear from me because of what I told about Gramps.* My role was to be sweet and cute. I would mask my feelings for the next several years.

My grade school teacher said on a report card, "Betsy is a delight to have in my class; however she is rather shy and seems unsure of herself."

One night I had a dream where I was laying on a wooden bed, and a Grinch like demon was hammering a huge stake into my feet. My feet were overlapping. I was screaming out for help in my dream, but with every swing of the mallet, the stake drove in deeper, and my voice became softer. The dream culminated in a shriek from the Grinch, and I awakened with my heart racing and a sweaty red face. My voice was silenced. I woke up in the dark and opened my mouth to scream. But nothing would come out.

The next morning we were heading back to Michigan with Gramps for the summer.

The first day after arriving in the land of Great Lakes, I proudly wore my crocheted white bikini. I had stitched it myself.

Gramps said, "Oh, you look so plump in that swimsuit." He was giving me a hard time because of our unspoken secret; *Those naptimes with Gramps.* I remember looking down at my twelve-year-old round belly and chubby thighs and thinking I was fat.

My favorite snack to sneak during summers at North Lake was several large spoonfuls of chocolate frosting from the soft Pillsbury jar that was kept in the old dishwasher turned storage bin. I had developed a penchant for chocolate.

That one little comment from my grandfather, "You look so plump in that swimsuit" would haunt me throughout my life. I developed issues over body image and food in High School, College and later as an adult.

Our Logan Scouting Family of Five

~Family Travels~

My parents did a great job of showing us three kids a sampling of the United States. We traveled to the Grand Canyon, Washington D.C., Hawaii, Puerto Vallarta- Mexico, New York, and of course Michigan every summer. One of my favorite trips was to the East Coast where we stayed in a super fancy hotel in New York. On Broadway, we saw the Rockettes kick their legs in unison high into the air. Then we shopped at Filene's Basement. I bought tube-tops and got a fun teenage New York wardrobe with my thirty dollars per month clothing allowance.

My mom and dad were very thoughtful and smart with money as their parents were raised in the Great Depression. They are very generous and very frugal all at the same time. So when we traveled, we had a mix of dinner and lodging at a fancy hotel, and then at night, we would sometimes separate the mattress from the box springs so Mark and Don would sleep right on the box springs while I had the luxurious mattress on the floor.

As the only daughter, there were a few perks. My parents honored my privacy as a girl, letting me sleep on a bed without my brothers. Separating the mattresses was a clever way to save money. We booked one hotel suite for all five of us. We were able to go on all of our great family trips because we often camped along the way or were *tight* with lodging and meals.

One time on my dad's birthday, we were traveling in New York, and we were going to surprise my dad with a birthday treat. My brothers and I were so excited to spring it on Dad. The treat was McDonald's specials for dinner! In those days, that was a huge treat, and we were always happy to split burgers, and shakes. French fries were an even bigger treat.

As we traveled we stopped at almost every tennis court, municipal golf course, or college track to get some exercise. Hiking and enjoying the birds and nature were part of the family routine as well. Dad was an avid birdwatcher.

One Christmas, we traveled to Hawaii with the whole family. Grandma and her dentures came too. During the trip, we stayed right next to the ocean in small cabins by the Black Sand Beach. One morning, Dad swam out to sea and almost did not return due to the strong riptides.

Another time years later, while touring Kauai in the car with my family, a giant five-inch spider appeared on my sixteen-year old brother's leg while he was driving. I was sitting in the front middle seat and Don flicked the spider right over me onto my brother Mark's lap! We all screamed, and as Don pulled off the road, Mark jumped out of the car window with the spider clinging to his shorts! Then the spider fell to the ground, poisonous fangs and all.

"Yikes! Where did that Tarantula come from?" Mark screeched, while kicking the giant creature with his tennis shoe.

"Must have been living in the engine of the rental car," Dad answered.

Through it all the family message was to stand tall; to 'grin and bear it.' We children learned not to complain and to overcome.

We were always well-fed and happy, and as the only girl in the family, I felt special growing up. As I grew into my teen years, I started to emerge from my cocoon of shyness.

Top: Brother Mark, Mom, Dad, me, Brother Don.
Bottom: Grandmother & Gramps Logan, Grandma Eckert.

~Boy Crazy~

"Let's, get, a little bit rowdy, R-O-W—D-Y!"

I cheered as our San Marcos High School football team pressed forward on the field. My short, royal blue cheerleader skirt revealed my suntanned legs, and my blonde frosted hair flung in the cold night air. I was a junior at San Marcos High School in Santa Barbara, and I thought I was "all that." I had just gotten my braces off, so I had straight white teeth. I liked boys and they seemed to like me too.

I had read in *Teen Magazine* that it was not okay to date more than three guys at a time in high school. While dating around quite a bit, I followed that rule and never had more than three guys calling me at a time. Then things changed.

Cheerleading for San Marcos High.

The summer before my senior year of high school, I started dating just one guy. Larry was a blonde-haired surfer. One warm June night Larry called and suggested we go for a drive. It was almost ten p.m., and my parents were already in bed, so I suggested instead that he come over to the house and we could "make-out" on the couch.

Larry replied, "Ok, I'll be right over, I really want to see you." Larry and I were kissing and whispering quietly on the couch in the living room in the dark.

I spoke softly, "This is so sneaky, my parents are asleep upstairs, and they have no idea you are here."

"Oh man! They are?" he whispered back.

Next, I heard the stairs creaking.

I breathed in his ear, "Stay here." I got up and tried to distract my Mom, who was walking down the stairs.

"Hi Mom, I'm getting a snack in the kitchen, want something?"

Mom said, "Oh, you're still up Bets. I'm just going to read a bit in the living room, and no snack now, thanks."

My cocky high school confidence started to slip.

"Ahhhhh!" my Mom screamed after she turned on the living room light and spotted Larry on the sofa. He was melting into the green tweed sofa as best as he could. All you could see were his startled blue eyes, like a deer in headlights. The date ended very quickly that night. Poor Larry.

A month later I was at the high school summer cheer-leading camp that was held at U.C.S.B. –University of California, Santa Barbara. Larry and I decided to hook-up in the parking lot and go for a drive, and I would ditch one of the boring camp assemblies. I carefully orchestrated the hook-up. When I spotted him in the parking lot, I ran and hopped in his car and we took off. Just when I thought we escaped without being caught, I noticed Mr. Madson, our bald-headed skanky cheer-leading director, chasing after us in his car yelling out the window.

I ducked in the car, and Larry said, "He's following us in his little green sports car. He is honking now too!"

My heart was pounding when Larry pulled over.

Mean ol' Madson rushed to the car window and yelled: "What are you doing Betsy!? You broke the rules of the cheer camp." He bellowed, "You're not allowed to leave the camp. The cheer squad will vote on what to do about this!"

I hopped out of the car and ran to the assembly in tears.

Poor Larry— that was the last time I saw him. I never heard from him again. Two weeks later, I was voted "off" the cheerleading squad by my *friends*.

I was devastated. My senior year in high school was shattered. Cheerleading and boys had been my life.

Thankfully my parents were encouraging, in fact throughout my childhood my dad would speak a positive affirmation over me, "Bets, you can do anything in life that you want to…you never get sick or down for long, you bounce right back." I would need those words later in life when larger trials came.

Dad was right, and the cheerleading event passed quickly. But I did turn to binge eating. I also forgot troubles by drinking at high school parties.

~After School Binging~

Afternoons were often spent at Esther's house. We made the most decadent after-school snacks. Sometimes we ate Mother's Double Fudge Cookies dipped in Cool Whip and cheese quesadillas fried in a puddle of butter with salt on top. We devoured entire bowls of chocolate-chip cookie dough. When in a pinch, we ate "Easy Bake" powdered cookie dough—just the dry powder.

One day, after eating an entire bowl of chocolate chip cookie dough, we decided to try throwing up in the bathroom.

"I feel absolutely disgusting." I said.

"My tummy really hurts this time." Esther replied.

As I shoved a finger down my throat, I gagged. My stomach churned and only a little spit-up landed in the toilet; just about one spoonful of cookie dough. We decided to lie down instead— moaning together for over an hour. Finally the discomfort passed.

When Esther's mom arrived home, she saw the dirty dishes, "Where are all the cookies?" she asked.

Esther and I guiltily replied together, "We just made a small batch and ate it all." We didn't reveal that we had tried to vomit. No one discussed bulimia or anorexia in the late seventies until the singer Karen Carpenter died.

Fun with Esther

~A Senior Bash~

January of my senior year in high school, I hatched a plan. I would host one of the best parties in San Marcos High history. It wasn't sanctioned by the school or my parents. It was at my home on Willow Glen Road in Santa Barbara.

While my parents were out of town for a week, I was in charge of the house. My parents trusted me. Several different friends stayed with me while my folks were gone. We passed out invitations, bought chips, dips and a few jugs of wine.

It was pretty easy to bat our eyelashes and have some older guy at a liquor store buy a few gallons of wine for us.

My parents said they would allow a party if there were just a dozen or so people with an adult present.

I charmed my friend's mom, Mrs. Laing into acting as a chaperone, "It's going to be a small party, and you can just read a book in one of the bedrooms." I told her.

That week, word of the party started getting around at school. My friends and I asked some of the football players to act as "bouncers" at the front door. I figured this would keep things in line, as I knew the party could get big.

The night of the party, my friend Candy arrived with the new release of the *Cars* album, *Candy-O*. With the music blaring loudly as friends and strangers arrived, I ushered Mrs. Liang into the back bedroom handing her a glass of cheap Tickle-Pink wine. We would not see her until the end of the party, and what a party it was.

The football bouncers left their post and joined in the festivities. In fact many of them began swimming in our pool while still wearing clothes. There was a large bubble dome over the pool kept inflated by an air blower. It worked well for year-round swimming. Almost everyone was drunk, and a few were hiding in the bushes smoking pot.

Suddenly there were shouts coming from the backyard,

"Let's jump off the roof onto the pool bubble!" the quarterback said. The huge linebackers lined up by a ladder and began jumping off the roof onto the pool bubble. I was sure that the bubble would explode, and I would be in huge trouble for sure. Inside the house people were dancing on the furniture as *Candy-O* droned over and over. *"Stairway to Heaven,"* by Led Zeppelin, was the only other record we owned besides my parent's classical collection. People began kissing each other randomly. Many had been vomiting in the yard just minutes before.

Then, while I danced in the living room, someone grabbed me, "The cops are here—they want to talk to an adult!"

Retrieving our unsuspecting chaperon from the bedroom, she sheepishly spoke with the police. The party was instantly over and now it was time to assess the damages. As friends left, the party goers could not find their purses or down-coats. Almost everyone at the party had received an expensive down coat for Christmas just a month before. Someone had cleaned us out. Thousands of dollars of coats were gone.

"At least none of my parents' things are missing," I said.

"None that you know of anyway," Ann replied.

You find out who your real friends are when it's time to clean up after an out-of-control bash. The next morning, I awoke Esther and Ann early to help me clean up the mess.

We filled bags and bags of bottles, cans, trash, pizza and partially-smoked marijuana joints found in the hedges.

Then my parents arrived home early from their trip. I thought everything was cool until I saw my mom talking with my least favorite neighbor, Mrs. King. She was using wild hand gestures to demonstrate our wild party. As Mom returned to the home, I knew there would be trouble.

"I will need to talk to you and Esther separately to find out what happened at this party—I feel betrayed," Mom said.

Immediately I snuck to the phone and called Esther to come and meet me at the corner. It was a "code one" parental emergency. "We better ride our bikes and meet on the corner." I whispered.

As Mom was busy giving a piano lesson, Esther and I formulated our plan of deception.

"My mom will be grilling us individually, so we better get our stories straight," I said.

That afternoon, I sat in the den across from my mom, "There were only about eighteen people at the party," I lied. My fingers were literally crossed behind my back as I rationalized *well maybe a hundred and eighteen*. I prayed that Esther would stick to the story or I would be grounded for months to come, and my parents would lose trust in me.

"I said exactly what we agreed on," Esther told me later. "About eighteen people."

Our only penalty was to bake chocolate chip cookies for the neighbors—including Mrs. King. A dozen at a time, we delivered them, tails between our legs.

I never saw myself as being an untruthful person, but during that season of my life, I wanted to stay out of trouble and keep my parents' trust in me.

I bounced back from being busted for the party, and being kicked off the cheerleading squad. I would now set my sights on the senior prom, graduation, and college.

Applying to several colleges, I was torn. Part of me wanted to stay at home in my comfortable Santa Barbara environment, attending City College. However, my parents thought I needed to broaden my horizons by going away to a known University.

They often said, "Ann Landers says, *healthy birds fly from the nest!*"

That fall, I found myself at a cute "Ivy League College of the West," known as U.O.P. ~University of the Pacific, in Stockton California. I quickly discovered it was more aptly named: "University Of Partying!"

~U.O.P. – "University of Partying"~

During college, there were lots of drugs and alcohol.

I tried a lot of stuff: Vodka punch, Cold Duck, daiquiris, beer bongs, lines, and pot. I'm sorry to say that I fell prey to so many of the temptations that a small private party school has to offer. I was in a sorority, Tri Delta, and met my future husband at college. We started dating the second week of my freshman year. I loved having a steady boyfriend and immediately threw myself into the relationship.

My college major was business with a psychology minor, though I focused more attention on the parties, sorority functions, and spending time with my boyfriend during the four years.

My sorority roommates and I struggled with food. We had gained the *Freshman Ten* as we loaded our plates with carbs and sweet treats at the dorm buffets lines. We weighed ourselves almost every day. I didn't want to get too plump because I wanted to be a cheerleader. It was a constant battle for me. One sorority sister arrived back to school an anorexic skeleton. Others of us would binge and diet, binge and diet. The first thing on my mind every morning was not school or my boyfriend, it was the scale. *Would I be a half pound less than the day before?* Binging on food was common, but over-drinking on the weekends was becoming a habit as well.

My senior year, I was a varsity cheerleader at UOP. Maybe there was some redemption and satisfaction in the fact that I was back on the football field cheerleading, doing cartwheels, sailor drops, and dangerous human pyramids after my experience in high school being kicked off the squad. There were just three gals and three guys on the cheer squad, so we did many tricky partner stunts with our guys.

My main cheer partner was a strong black fellow named "Bird." He was tall and lanky, and held my leg tight as he thrust my muscular body into the crisp fall air. When I was cheering, my mind was only on the game and our cheers. All other concerns like homework, relationship issues, my weight, parties, clothes, jealousies, and money vanished as I leapt from one pose to the next.

UOP College Cheerleader ~ Go Tigers!

~Headaches on Campus~

One UOP fraternity party stands out in particular. The guys were serving "Everclear-punch." Everclear is a transparent alcohol that is odorless, tasteless, and has a super high alcohol content of 92%. There may be no alcohol in existence that is more potent. The guys had traveled to Nevada to get the stuff. The sole purpose was to make a fruit punch that the sorority gals would drink, like, and not taste the alcohol, thereby getting us very drunk.

Well the strategy worked on both the guys and gals. One guy was found the next morning passed out in the bushes. Another guy that passed out on the stairs of the fraternity awoke with one of his eyebrows shaved off. Several of my sorority sisters vomited, and I suffered a severe headache and nausea. While at the party, one of the frat brothers offered to take me and my friend on a tour of the three story Tudor style fraternity house.

"I'll show you ladies the sleeping porch, the attic, and we can raid the kitchen!" he exclaimed.

And as we walked through the sea of empty bunk beds on the sleeping porch, I heard a low soft moan. There was a guy lying on the bottom bunk of one bed, and he was foaming at the mouth. It oozed down his cheek. I walked closer.

"Are you ok?" I asked in a soft voice.

There was no answer. I poked him gently on the arm. There was no response. The nerdy frat brother showing us around said,

"He'll be ok."

I said, "I think we need to call an ambulance."

"But what about raiding the kitchen?" he urged.

After a bit of discussion, we called 911 and he was taken to the ER by ambulance. I heard the next day that his blood alcohol level was so high that he should have died for sure.

That weekend I realized that *I could speak up,* and that somehow speaking the truth and doing the right thing could even help save a life.

It started to feel like a calling on my life, to speak the truth in the face of adversity.

Soon I would be entering a new chapter in my life after graduating from UOP in Stockton, California. The party would continue at my wedding ceremony with me and my college boyfriend of four years. At the age of 21, my life was changing, beginning with those two famous words...

~Married at Twenty-One~

"I do," I said, as I looked at my newly betrothed husband, who sported a black tuxedo and a summer suntan. My mom's wedding dress hung snugly on my slimmed down 112 pound frame, and my "Farrah Fawcett" hair-do engulfed my carefully made-up face. We were fresh out of college and ready for the world.

For several years, we lived the country club lifestyle in Oakland, then in Piedmont California before having kids. I enjoyed large diamond rings, expensive vacations, fancy cars, and a membership at the elite local country club. On the weekends we all attended parties with the mayor and pastors of Piedmont, drinking vintage wines, laughing loudly past midnight, and oftentimes driving home with a good buzz, if not drunk. There were nearly ten years of this lifestyle before the babies arrived.

~Jennifer and Katelyn~

Birthing a baby is a miracle. In my case I had two natural born miracles within fifteen months.

During the excruciating pain of labor, there was no way to know the reward ahead. At Alta Bates birthing center on a hot July night, I screamed, "Ohhhh! Please give me some pain killers!"

My severe birthing pain approached twenty hours, "I can't take it!"

Now I know why they are called *Labor* Nurses. My nurse's specialty seemed to be in pain and *hard labor*.

Smiling in her purple scrubs, she matched my loud moans, "You can do this Betsy! —Think of your grandmothers and ancestors doing this over the centuries without *any* medication!" She twirled around the room with a needle in her hand trying to distract me. "You are almost there! Hang in there—the baby's crowning right now!"

Just when I thought I would die, my baby popped out. There was my beautiful daughter, Jennifer. As she nursed at my bosom, I was instantly in love. The pain was immediately forgotten.

The second time around, just 14 months later, I screamed again for painkillers. The same nurse in purple scrubs smiled and started in about the ancestors who had babies naturally in the past. Before I could even cry out for an epidural, I was holding another new precious life, her name was Katelyn. I fell in love again as she blinked her eyes at me and cuddled in. When all the drama was over, I was grateful for the nurse in purple.

Jenny and Katie instantly became *the apple of my eye* and I devoted myself to being a good mommy. My mom had taught me how important bonding the first few years of life is for children, so I made an extra effort to spend the bulk of my time with them. I breast-fed each daughter for nearly a year. In fact breast feeding was such a special time for me as I rocked my babies and finally got a few minutes to relax and connect.

I pushed them to the park in the side-by side double stroller every day, and we read them bedtime stories every night before prayers. Favorite books were, *I'll love you Forever* and *Everyone Poops*. And my favorite: *Take time to Relax*.

Little Jenny and Katie

As the girls got older, we often went with our puppy, Bagpipes, to see the "Cookie Lady." At her story book home they munched on cookies and heard colorful stories from this petite eighty-year-old neighbor. The Cookie Lady, Lena, was well known in Piedmont, and was often featured in the "Piedmont Post," the local paper, as being such a special generous lady, who was full of spunk and vinegar. She would *tell it like it is!* I was so drawn to this wise old lady; we would stay in touch for years to come.

For me at home though, in the fast-paced competitive San Francisco Bay Area, stress was ramping up. I tried to be the "perfect" mother, wife, part-time interior designer, and "keep up with the Joneses." Our debts were building, our marriage was suffering, and we were slapped with a huge IRS audit. I felt overwhelmed by the demands of life and I was exhausted. Our daughters took center stage for me. They were my refuge. I only worked a couple days a week as an interior designer, yet there were never enough hours in the day. *"A mother's work is never done,"* and it seemed like I was *"Dancing as fast as I can."*

~Baby Stephanie~

When the girls were one and two, I found myself pregnant again. I prayed for a miscarriage since I was so run-ragged, and our marriage was unstable just under the pretty surface. I considered an abortion since I felt so alone and overwhelmed. Every day was a struggle for me. I often drank at night to drown out my feelings.

It was *not* a good time to have another child. My husband traveled so much for business, I felt alone in the marriage.

"Should I have an abortion?" I asked my pastor, my friends and husband. There was subtle pressure to "get rid" of this unwanted pregnancy. It was haunting me that the baby's fingers were starting to develop.

One wise friend said, "Betsy, what does your heart say?" My heart said not to get rid of this baby, but my mind was trying to dominate.

Then my friend asked, "How do you separate your heart and head?"

Should I have an abortion? I thought.

As I tossed and turned in bed that night, a *still small voice* echoed inside of me. It was a powerful answer:

"No—no abortion. Stick it out."

Then sitting up in bed, I repeated, "No! Stick it out!"

I believed this message was right from God.

So stay the course I did. It was time to dig deep for the baby in my womb. The torment lifted.

Everyone in the family began to get excited about our third child. Would we have a "Stephanie" or "Stephen?" We talked about adding a bedroom to our gingerbread home in Piedmont. I dreamed of having three little children to love and cuddle. There is a supernatural excitement that happens when women are pregnant. It overshadows problems. The girls started to share my delight. It was a happy couple of months.

My friend Susan, across the street said I started to "glow" as the bulge in my belly grew. I hid the hardship, mistrust and disconnect in the marriage.

Unfortunately, I did not nurture myself or the unborn baby. My diet and drinking were not healthy. I cooked the "SAD Diet" the: **S**tandard **A**merican **D**iet. It was the easy way to go with young children. A diet filled with carbs, sugars, and bad fats; pizza, mac and cheese and microwave dinners. Trying to stay away from wine was my biggest struggle. My unborn baby ate what I ate, thought what I thought, and drank what I drank during those six months, until one fateful day at the OB/GYN doctor.

★★★★★

I was staring at the ultra sound screen in disbelief. The doctor pressed harder on my belly with the probe trying to get a response from the baby. She wasn't moving. I saw the frozen skeleton of my precious baby, curled up in a ball. *Why wasn't she moving? Where was her heartbeat?* I was almost six months pregnant with a third baby girl, in for a routine ultrasound on a Friday afternoon.

Sparing the doctor having to tell me the bad news, I said, "Something is wrong, isn't it?"

He nodded as he continued to glide the K-Y lubricated probe over the protrusion in my belly. I could feel the bones of my baby pressing through the layers of my womb, my muscles and skin. My baby was motionless, and I realized she was not alive.

My baby was dead, and I was responsible for her death.

What was the punishment for a mother like me? I thought.

The doctor informed me then that I would have to carry this dead baby in my belly until a procedure could be scheduled.

Now my guilt and shame began. I had wished for a miscarriage early in my pregnancy because I was so overwhelmed. Many nights I drained half a bottle of Chardonnay during the pregnancy. There were evening hot tubs for stress. There were very few leafy greens or vegetables on our plates. There were strong antibiotics when I had the flu. And I had actually considered aborting my unborn child. *Did my baby sense this?*

The struggle with my increasingly unhealthy marriage of thirteen years completely overwhelmed me. I felt out-of- touch with God and myself.

Only weeks before this disaster, we had decided to rally behind the pregnancy and add this new baby to our family. We chose names, bedding and paint and told all of our friends and family the exciting news...

Shall I spare you the details of the resulting labor and delivery of my baby? I was scheduled for a procedure called a dilation and extraction, a D and E, on the Wednesday after the ultrasound to "extract" the dead baby. I had to carry her in my belly for five days before the procedure, *dead*. I remember going to Marine World with my two living daughters and a few friends and pretending like everything was fine as I carried the "still" child in my womb. I know it sounds crazy, walking around a theme park with a dead baby in my belly, but I was in denial.

The night before the scheduled procedure, I awoke at 2 a.m. with excruciating pain. Was I in labor? What was going on? I knew that something was horribly wrong. We called the doctor. The doctor said to go back to sleep, that it was just false labor. The pain persisted and grew increasingly worse. Finally in desperation I begged to be taken to the emergency room at Alta Bates Hospital in Berkeley.

We took our two daughters to the neighbor's house and raced to the hospital. Blood was leaking out of me all over the seats of our pristine white BMW. The baby's head was pressing to come out of me. I pushed her back in with both hands, not wanting to deliver a dead baby in the car. Both the baby and I needed a shred of dignity. Screaming in physical and emotional pain, I was rushed into the emergency room on a stretcher.

The doctor finally showed up, and I whimpered, "Shall I push?"

"It doesn't really matter," he said.

No one wants to deliver a dead baby, I thought.

Then she was born still and lifeless in the emergency room at Alta Bates Hospital, at 3:15 a.m. I was devastated. My heart was bleeding tears, and I felt my life had come to an end along with hers.

The nurse placed my stillborn child in a mauve plastic, rectangular tub, and asked if we wanted to see her. I whimpered a soft, "yes." She was curled up tight with her head bowed and her little hands pulled together like she was praying. *So beautiful.* I cried softly in resignation as they took her away in the sterile shoebox tub. There was no respect for this child, my Baby Stephanie.

The loss of this child left me with a hole in my heart. It was my job to take care of this unborn baby. She was depending on me, and I let her down.

~Remorse~

I often woke up at 3 a.m. with a tear-soaked pillowcase. I cried for months. Soon I developed night terrors, jolting awake at all hours of the darkness anxious about my children. Several times I found myself sleepwalking, even running downstairs to check on the imaginary baby I was dreaming about.

One time I tripped on the stairs and fell all the way to the bottom of the flight, awakening to my sick feeling of loss. Even though I had been overwhelmed with the idea of another baby, the loss of her was immense. It was hard on my husband and daughters as they missed her too and also watched me suffer and cry so often.

I took care of my family during the day and smiled as best as I could, but I felt tormented. My life was lived in quiet anguish and desperation just under the pristine exterior.

During this season in my life, I started taking anti-depressants and continued drinking to numb my pain. The anti-depressants I tried, Lexapro and Paxil, caused me go back to sleep until noon, and strangely, I found myself smiling sometimes when something was sad. These psychotropic pharmaceutical drugs made me even more depressed. I wished that I had died, not my sweet baby, but I had two children, a husband, and dog at home. Life must go on, yet how?

The guilt was horrific from my heavy drinking, poor diet, my prior desire for a miscarriage, and extreme stress during the pregnancy. I read somewhere that the alcohol we drink when pregnant goes straight into the baby's bloodstream. The tiny liver is not developed enough to filter out the toxins; therefore it can cause different issues for the fetus...sometimes fatal, sometimes birth defects.

I was down on myself for my poor choices during the pregnancy, and I knew between me and God that my decisions affected the pregnancy. I now understand that anger turned inward is depression, and I had turned my anger inward.

My life felt like an open wound...with salt poured on it. I mourned the loss of Baby Stephanie, and I also mourned the loss of part of my childhood innocence due to the sexual abuse from my Gramps.

They say when you grieve one loss, you grieve them all, so grieve I did. The black days stretched on into the summer, fall, and winter.

~Forgiven Forever~

One spring morning there would be a major turning point in my life. It was a year after the loss of Baby Stephanie, and we were attending our community church, keeping up appearances. It was communion Sunday, but this Sunday would be different.

Typically, there were dry round wafers for communion, but this particular morning there were torn pieces of bread. As I sat somberly in the wooden pew, I raised the bread and cup slowly to my mouth and took them both in. All at once I heard a sweet angelic voice ring out from high in the choir loft, *"Then sings my soul, my Saviour God to Thee!"* It was my favorite soloist, Mary.

At that very moment, I remembered in my heart that God loves me, and Jesus died on the cross for my sins, and I was forgiven! *I was forgiven!* Tears streamed down my mascara streaked face. At that very moment I knew God's forgiveness gave me a fresh start. I knew that my baby was in a wonderful place and I would see her again in Heaven someday.

As I wept, I joined in a hushed tone to the final stains of the hymn; *"Then I shall bow with humble adoration, And then proclaim, my God, How Great Thou Art!"*

~A New Life~

That day, I started over as a brand new person.

After this spiritual renewal, I found that the country club, fine jewelry, glitzy vacations, and partying lifestyle were not working for me anymore. My life seemed shallow, somewhat hollow. I longed for a simpler life. I longed for inner peace. I longed for meaning in my life. Even though there was this major turning point in my life, for some reason, I still found myself drinking several glasses of chardonnay most nights, often alone. At this point in my journey, wine was still my best friend.

As I recovered from the loss of Baby Stephanie, and accepting God's forgiveness, I dug deep. I continued the process of grief with all the stages—denial, anger, despair, sorrow, acceptance, and then receiving grace, hope, love, and forgiveness. There was a choice each day. I could continue to live my life the way I had in the past, and suffer from anxiety and depression because of the life that I was living, or I could take a leap of faith and align my life and choices with my new found truths and beliefs.

I realized that the gap between the life that I was living and the life that my heart told me to live was far too great.

It would be a concerted effort to embrace joy as often as possible; taking time to exercise, be still, and to meditate on scripture daily. I simplified my life and schedule. I vowed to do better with false pretenses and gossip. I even sold some of my fancy jewelry.

Other priorities changed after that. I joined a Bible study, centering prayer/meditation group, and Stephen Ministry training. With the support of family, friends, a Christian counselor, church, and the grace of God, I was able to grow, to embrace life. As I moved forward in freedom, I felt grateful. I was forgiven. A week later I went off antidepressants too. *I wanted Jesus to be my antidepressant.*

~Rollerblading with a Tambourine~

That summer, I began rollerblading around Lake Merritt, in downtown Oakland, shaking a tambourine. On the big round tambourine I wrote with my thickest Sharpie:

"Jesus Loves Us!"

Then I started passing out Little Bibles to street people around the lake. There was rebirth, and I wanted others to know there was a free gift of forgiveness and eternal life for them too. I felt alive, exchanging stories with homeless people.

Passing out Little Bibles

The loss of Baby Stephanie brought me back to Jesus. I'm sorry that my baby's life needed to be lost to get me back in the fold with God, but I guess some of us are more stubborn than others. I was so grateful. I was on a spiritual high.

Back at home it wasn't all so blissful, as my husband wondered what was going on with me. I heard, "Just don't become a born-again-Christian." But I *was* new, and my life was changing. I remembered the saying, "Men marry women hoping they will never change. Women marry men hoping to change them."

Sometimes men cope with unwanted change by just checking out. But for me, faith was the only thing keeping me afloat.

One night after rollerblading and passing out Little Bibles, I lay in bed alone and read, *"Though your sins are like scarlet, I will make them white as snow."* (Isaiah 1:18)

~Baby Flowers~

A few years after the loss, Jenny and Katie and I were at the Mountain View Cemetery visiting Baby Stephanie's gravestone and having a picnic. The girls, five and six years old, were romping on the hillside, as I sat by Stephanie's memorial stone.

All of a sudden Jenny came running to me and said, "Mommy come quick and see. There are the most beautiful baby flowers over here; I think Baby Stephanie sent them to us!" Sure enough there were delicate "lacy weeds" among the cemetery grass.

"Yes," I said. "Look at the itty-bitty yellow star shaped flowers."

"They have pretty little white centers," Katie chimed in.

To this day, when I see tiny flowering weeds with blue, peach, yellow or white flowers, I wistfully think of Baby Stephanie and what a gift she has been to me and my girls; an angel. She reminds me of the promise of heaven.

Picnics visiting Baby Stephanie.

41

I love that about God. He offers us such good stuff—forgiveness, heaven, peace.

Through trials and blessings, I found life is chalked with good and bad things. Life is like a railroad track with two rails. On one rail there are good things happening, and on the other there are bad things. They often occur simultaneously.

Maybe it is not so much what transpires in our lives, but how we respond. I felt encouraged to respond with faith in God's plan, open to spiritual growth and change. Several scriptures gave me great hope during this transformational time:

"You made all the delicate inner parts of my body, and knit them together in my mother's womb" (Psalms 139: 13)

"Cast your burden upon the Lord and he shall sustain you." (1 Peter 5:7)

"Therefore if anyone is in Christ, he is a new creation; the old has gone, the new has come!" (2 Corinthians 5:17)

Traveling by train with the girls along the coast of California. Mom sees us off at the station

The Gramps Letters~

Being renewed and deciding to trust God with my life opened my eyes in many ways, and I realized that I needed to come to terms with my childhood and work on forgiveness with my family. Gramps was dead and gone by the time I was in my mid-thirties, with two young daughters. I decided to volunteer to help children.

While taking classes to learn more about child sexual abuse, I began teaching at CAP, Child Abuse Prevention. I was teaching communication skills to kindergartners. We did puppet shows to show what kind of touching is not okay. We encouraged children to talk to a trusted adult if there was something going on in their life that did not seem right.

We also encouraged them *not* to keep secrets, to tell a trusted parent or teacher if a teen or adult asked them to *keep a secret* or *touched them* on their private parts. We asked them to find a buddy at school if they were being bullied or hurt by another kid.

While teaching child abuse prevention, the memories of my own childhood sexual abuse came back to haunt me. As an adult, I would need to dig deep, struggle with what had happened, and offer forgiveness to those involved.

One day before teaching the kindergartners, I remembered back to when I was just six years old. I had said to my cousin, Cindy, "Gramps touches me during naptime."

Cindy had responded, "Yeah he does that with me too…but I try and stop him."

At the time, it helped me to know I was not alone. He did things to her too. I was glad my Mom believed me when I had told her what Gramps did during naps when I was a little girl.

There were quite a few incidents of Gramps' fondling that I remembered, and over the years I remembered more and more.

There was a *conspiracy of silence* throughout the country when I was growing up regarding sexual abuse, and my family and I were not excluded.

I learned that people sometimes repeat the same type of abuse that happened to them. I was later told that while Gramps was growing up in Argentina as a missionary kid, he was sexually fondled at naptime by his nannies.

As an adult, I would need to grapple with how to best protect and inform my daughters about the ever present threat of sexual abuse.

Studies showed that more than one in four girls and one in six boys are sexually molested. I wanted to help make a difference now that I was a grown adult, and share the truth of what happened to me.

After careful consideration, I decided to reach out to some female cousins and neighbors who spent time with Gramps in Michigan while we were growing up. I sent out a letter to several of them. My hope was to give them the same relief that I felt as a little girl after talking to my six year old cousin. She had told me that *Gramps did stuff to her too.*

I wanted them to know that if they were abused, they were not alone. There would be closure for me, as I dropped the letters in to the mailbox.

Here is the letter I sent:

Dear Precious Cousin,

I hope you are well. I think of you often, and smile at the good times we shared during the summers in Michigan on North Lake.

I am writing today to let you know what happened to me as a child with Gramps. When I was three to six years old Gramps touched me many times inappropriately during naps and piggy back rides and in the pool. Now I am working through things in counseling. Part of my process of moving forward, is communicating with women who spent time with him as a child. I hope that nothing happened to you when you were with Gramps. In case it did, please know that you are not alone.

I did speak with someone else who had a similar experience with Gramps. For some reason, it helped me knowing that I was not the only one that he fondled.

There is a light at the end of the tunnel of grief and sadness. I have learned to forgive.

Please feel free to call or email me anytime if you want to talk. I am sending good wishes, lots of love, and God's Blessings,

Love, Your Cousin, Betsy

I sent this letter to several, and called a few others. Through this process, I found that there were many others fondled by Gramps. I also did some counseling with my husband at the time, and even a session with my parents to help restore health to our relationships and offer up forgiveness. My parents apologized. My dad had felt that it might cause more harm to make a big ordeal out of it back then. My mom did her best to protect me from Gramps after I told her. And it was not socially acceptable to talk about these things. I forgave them as best as I could.

Then my mom reached out to several other family members in Michigan, telling the truth of what happened in a well-written letter. I appreciated that. I also wrote a letter to my mom.

~Letter to Mom~

Dear Mom,

You've been a great Mom... You taught me so many valuable lessons over the years—

I know that we have both had a hard time dealing with all of the issues surrounding "Gramps." I am so proud of you and the letter you wrote and sent to my Uncles and other older relatives about what happened when I was a little girl, and how Gramps touched me inappropriately.

I am now a survivor, and yes Mom I forgive you ...thank you for apologizing.

I once heard;

"The thing that awakens the deepest fountain of gratitude in a human being is that God has forgiven our sin."

God forgave me for my mistakes, so I am called to forgive others. You are a wonderful mom. I forgive you and I will always love you.

Love, Betsy

P.S. I'll never forget how you always helped me with my book reports and helped me get my arms straight for cheerleading tryouts!

There were a variety of reactions to my phone calls and letters. One Michigan neighbor that I called, mentioned that she and her sister were also inappropriately touched by Gramps. "At first, I didn't think it was so bad—but then as things went on it started to hurt a bit." She said.

"Oh, that's so sad," I said, "You know after I told my parents, the subject was never brought up again. I think it stopped after that though."

She said that she told her mother about it when she was little, and her mother said, "Oh no, that is not possible. He would never do that!"

Her Mom's reaction at the time would silence her. She told me that her sister never trusted men after being fondled. But Bev was happily married and had dealt with the issue. Then she sent me a picture of her family and a book on prayer.

Phoning another relative, I shared what happened to me. I asked if I could share with their grown daughter, because I heard she took "naps" with Gramps as a child.

The response was very short, "We want to remember him in a good way." Interesting how people often "shoot" the messenger.

It was not me doing the molesting, yet by some folks' reaction, you would think I was the one who committed the crime. Not only was the anger often misplaced, but that fierce conspiracy of silence would shut down discussions. The stubborn silence blocked growth and healing. If people *pretended* that it never happened, then that would make it so.

For me there was an inner-determination to address my past and present hurts and to grow from them— to tell the truth in the face of adversity and denial. When an abuser is still around we are called to do something about it. We are called to shine light onto the darkness and expose evil deeds. We draw firm boundaries to protect children. We are also called to forgive.

~Escape to the Isle of Skye~

At this point after this huge conversion in my life, becoming aware of freedom through forgiveness, it affected my home life, but not in a good way. Every mother can relate to screaming toddlers running around the home, and there was other screaming in my home as well.

As I grew in my faith, I started to draw healthy boundaries and speak the truth with love more. As a result my home life was being pushed right to the brink. I needed some time to contemplate. How could my faith change my marriage so much? I needed to search for answers. Life was getting out of control and the drinking had escalated. There was an angry and mistrustful spirit in our home.

My good friend from college, Cheryl, lived and worked as a school teacher in Great Britain.

One day she called me from Great Britain, "Hi Betsy, do you want to come visit me over here in Scotland?"

I grabbed the opportunity, scraped money together, and hopped on a plane to Liverpool. I needed a break. My parents pitched in with some money and offered to watch the girls while I was gone.

Arriving in England, the rental car had a stick shift on the left side. How would it work backwards? Now I was by myself, driving on the wrong side of the road from the wrong side of the car. The rain began pouring buckets as I left the airport grinding my sporty green Mini Cooper. I could not even find the windshield wipers in this backwards car. Then I circled the round-about, and my tires and hubcaps were "buzzing" the curb! I became lost at night in the downpour, and my tears began to flow as well. I hadn't slept in two days. As I followed my little airport map toward the Isle of Skye, I felt so lost and alone that I pulled the car to the side of the muddy country road. The following half hour I sat in my rental car like a wounded animal.

Then by a miracle a young couple pulled over, "Need some help missy?"

I wiped my tears away and said, "Thanks – I've lost my way to the Isle of Skye."

The sweet couple helped bolster my spirits and then provided directions to the island.

The next morning at my British island bed and breakfast, a day of renewal began. I thanked God for getting me to my destination safely. The next few days, before going to visit Cheryl, I spent doing the most life affirming solo activities I could think of, hiking, eating the healthiest British food I could find, watercolor painting, visiting castles, journaling, and most of all just resting.

Through this break from the hectic lifestyle, I began to feel empowered and renewed. What a relief it was from the emotional roller coaster back home in the States. I realized for the first time that I was capable of defining my own path; reclaiming joy in life.

Then, I visited Cheryl where she was a teacher in Scotland. I gave a little talk to her third-grade class. They were filled with laughter after hearing my funny American accent.

Getaway to Isle of Skye and Paris. Meeting sorority sister, Cheryl ~ Sampling Parisian Dark Chocolate!

Then Cheryl and I went to Paris for a few days where we were the consummate tourists. We ate, drank, shopped, and visited museums like the Louvre. My favorite part of Paris was simply sampling all of the sumptuous chocolate. I couldn't wait to get home to see my daughters, share some chocolate, and try out some new recipes. I vowed to return home with a refreshed spirit.

~Martha, Julia and Betty Crocker~

Back home in Piedmont, my married life was falling apart. After my time in Europe, I felt even more alone.

I still relished raising my daughters Jennifer and Kate. Like most mothers, I instinctively knew how important it was to shape their mind, heart, and soul. At one point, I seriously considered home-schooling the girls. We would have had more time together. I wish I grabbed that opportunity.

As the girls were growing up at our charming English cottage home in Piedmont near San Francisco, I tried to make things fun for them. I was self-employed, working part time as an interior designer for friends and clients in the East Bay. Working one project at a time allowed me more time to spend with our daughters. I loved being the mom to drive on the field trips. I also taught a "friendship class" in Katie's second grade. There was specialized training to teach Jennifer's fifth grade PEP class. It dealt with communication skills, refusal skills, dangers of drugs and alcohol addiction, and bullying.

One time I spent my own money to buy an alcohol "pickled liver" and a lung from a smoker that had died. You should have seen the look of the students faces as they passed around the damaged organs. On one side of the box was the healthy pink colored organ, and on the other was the sickly one. The booze damaged liver looked like a large black bumpy pickle, I will never forget it. I tried to slow down on my drinking, but it still had quite a stronghold on me. A better obsession was cooking and food.

One of my favorite things to do at home with the girls was to cook together. We made Rocky Mountain Chip cookies and cabbage soup. We made seven-layer pizza burger, Jouzits, spaghetti, banana bread and Olallieberry pies with berries from our lush bush in the back yard.

When the girls were young, they were adept at using sharp knives to chop vegetables into pieces the size of "Skittles." Our favorite cake to bake for birthdays was Chocolate Mayonnaise Cake. Sounds strange, but it is delicious and moist. As we baked, we often pretended that we were famous chefs on a live cooking show, Julia Childs, Martha Stewart, and Betty Crocker...

"Look at the beautiful color of the cake batter!" Jennifer exclaimed in her best shrill British accent.

"Yes, and let me show the viewing audience how to stir in the secret ingredient, mayonnaise, for this yummy cake!" Kate said using her biggest grown-up voice.

And me, as Betty Crocker, exclaiming with my eyebrows raised, "Let's pour the cake batter into the pans, so we can all eat cake soon!"

Kate and Jen would always add, "And let's all have one sample of the batter first, just to make sure it is good!" We all giggled as we carefully spooned out a sample of the chocolate batter and licked our spoons clean.

I was in heaven when I was cooking with my pretty little daughters. Teaching my girls how to cook and have fun, just like I did with my mom.

I share a few of my favorite recipes at the end of this book as a reward to the reader for making it through all of this with me.

~Affairs of the Heart~

Over the next several years I would try to make the best of my home life for my children. I felt lonely in the marriage and suffered with suspicion and anxiety.

I found solace in taking the girls to the park or visiting the cookie lady, who always had wonderful wisdom and colorful stories. She often said to me, "What the heck does all that worrying do for you Betsy? Just give it to God." Even though my heart was for God, I would not escape the temptations of the world.

My part-time work in San Francisco with interior design projects was a welcome break from the hectic pressures of home life. I often felt like a single mother as my husband took so many business trips. There was an escape besides work that also attracted me.

There is a phenomenon that women don't talk about much, especially married women, where we start to have romantic thoughts about other men. I found myself in situations at work where I was fantasizing about being in a relationship. I would day-dream about a coworker or businessman client while helping decorate their office. Everything looks romantically rosy at work, away from the dirty dishes, laundry, bills and stinky diapers.

Everyone has heard of the office romance, right? There are provocative outfits and dapper business suits. We had fancy lunches together in the name of business, often sipping wine with someone before hopping on the Bart train home. We return home to the same old day-to-day problems.

I came up with a name for this very common trend. I called these feelings, *"Affairs of the Heart."* Unlike some of my co-workers, I never crossed the line physically but did mentally and emotionally. Because of my flirtatious ways, men would often cross the line with me during this time of fantasy and work.

~Zip, Zip, Zip...~

One time my boss, George, called me to help him with inventory in the basement of the design warehouse. In this case, I hadn't even been fantasizing about him and respected the fact that he was married. I probably was too friendly, and he read it the wrong way. So when we were alone in the dark basement, checking off the quantities of furniture on my inventory clipboard, I was shocked to hear the sound of a zipper opening and closing in my direction several times. *"Zip, Zip... Zip, Zip."* I began to panic when I realized my boss was busy exposing himself to me!

Yikes, this was my employer, I thought. I took a deep breath, stood tall in my navy skirt and white ruffle blouse and decided to ignore the behavior. I became very businesslike, and eventually he stopped the zipping. Then without a word I gathered my papers and clipboard and left the basement.

Another time, I gave some flowers to a male client and took him to lunch, hoping that he would order all of their furniture through me. I thought he was handsome in his pinstriped suit, but we were both married. After lunch we went back to his office, and he started to tell me about his photography work.

"I want to take some private pictures of you," he said.

"Right now?" I asked.

I was hopeful to get the furniture deal and a big commission.

"My specialty is in topless and nude photography," my client said as he swiveled to the credenza grabbing a large camera. On the desk there was a picture of his wife and baby.

As I sat in his sky rise office, I felt my face flush and his eyes looked right through me. I quickly made up an excuse to get back to my office "for a meeting." *What was I doing?* I thought. *I don't need the commission that bad.*

I did stop short of any physical adultery but felt guilty for my fantasy world. Later I read that when you look lustfully at someone you may as well have committed adultery with them. *Oh my.* With my behavior, I became very suspicious of my husband. In marriage counseling, I could not confront him on anything, because I had a secret life myself.

All of the mistrust, drinking, chaos, and financial issues with the marriage, gave me a longing to get away from it all once again. So when my mom offered to pay for a trip to a mountain top retreat in Italy, I was already packing my bags. Back to Europe, lucky me.

~Monte Oliveto with my Mom - a retreat to Italy~

I was finding solace in daily centering prayer and peaceful Christian retreats during this season of my life. The prayer retreat was held at a fifteenth century Benedictine Monastery high on a mountaintop in Tuscany. The old Benedictine monks still made jam and bread there. It would be one full week of complete silence. There would be no talking at all. It was considered a silent retreat.

It was very peaceful and powerful at the same time. Once again, I would be taking a lot of walks alone and contemplating God, His love, and my lonely yet hectic and codependent life back home.

One of the yoga instructors at the retreat was an Italian stallion, Giovanni; dark skin, dark hair, white toothy smile and a yoga body. All the women had a crush on him, including me. Here I was at a Holy Monastery, high on a mountain in Italy, and I was having another "affair of the heart."

Not only did I break that rule, but in the midst of this holy and silent adventure, Mom and I broke down. We talked. In fact we laughed; an even bigger no-no. It was late at night past bedtime and curfew, when all the lights were out. My mother and I just couldn't take it anymore, as we sat on our dorm style beds, we laughed for five minutes straight. I can't remember what it was about; maybe it was the funny expression on mom's face every time she opened or closed the ancient dresser drawers. Maybe it was about not talking at all, but we laughed until we cried.

The next morning, rising early for the six a.m. prayer time, the monk in charge broke the silence and told the whole group that, "There were some guests causing a disturbance in the East wing of the monastery last night."

My mom looked at me with a startled look, and I bit my tongue hard to keep from laughing again.

On the plane ride home I would not be laughing. Once able to really open up and talk, after being silent and prayerful for almost a week, I broke down and talked with my Mother about the troubles at home. My marriage was crumbling, and I was finally able to admit it. My mom understood. She became very compassionate and talked it through with me. When I stepped off the plane into the San Francisco fog, I knew my life would be changing forever.

~End of a Marriage ~ End of a Dream~

Walking through the door of our gingerbread home in Piedmont, nothing had changed. Behind our closed doors there were the "three A's," anger, alcohol, and abandonment. There are three other "A's" that poison a marriage; adultery, addictions, and abuse. But at that point it seemed we weren't even working on the marriage anymore. I tried hard to keep up appearances for the children, neighbors, and friends until the bitter end.

Lonesomeness, anger and distrust consumed me as my husband traveled so much for his work, and deep down I wondered what he was doing on those trips. I think he was upset that I had changed, and I had. I had found Jesus and wanted to make Him first place in my life. I wanted Jesus to be first place in all of our lives. In some ways it must have been hard on my marriage partner of so many years, when I began to live with a different set of values. Our several years of marriage counseling had still not resolved the issues.

In my family growing up, divorce was not considered to be an option, so I had tried like heck to make it work. I lived with such high anxiety that insidious physical disease had set into my body, and I didn't even know it.

One stormy winter night as I lay awake alone, I reached for a book of Bible promises someone had given me. I looked up divorce. "God hates divorce," I read. *I hate divorce too*, I thought. Divorce was a last resort for me. Then I found a commentary that said, "Jesus' exceptions for divorce do not constitute an excuse to escape a difficult marriage, however in some cases may liberate those who genuinely tried to save their marriage…" I also found a verse in 1 Corinthians Chapter seven that talked about allowing for divorce in the case of abandonment. Then I pleaded with God for guidance that rainy night. Alone in the bed, I matched the wild storm with my sobbing. Finally the rain stopped. In my heart I knew the tears from heaven had poured out, and like those raindrops, I was now finally released.

It was one of the saddest days of my life when we told Jenny and Katie, on a picnic, that their Mommy and Daddy were getting divorced. Their Daddy would be moving to an apartment. We all cried and cried.

My main goal in life to that point was to be a good mom and wife. I felt that I had failed my marriage and my daughters. Next was the tragic manipulative tug-of-war over custody of the girls for years to follow.

After seventeen years of marriage, I was no longer a married woman. I was Betsy, a divorcee, mother of Jennifer and Katie. And I would need to pull myself together and focus on just being a good mom.

~No Child Left with Time~

In the heat of the divorce, I did not realize that I would have so much less time with the girls. They would be spending time away from home with their dad, in addition to the demands of school, homework and soccer. School in the fancy town of Piedmont was all about competition, grades, tests and being the prettiest and best.

When my girls were in middle school and high school, the homework they had was overwhelming. I was so upset that they had so much school work sent home with them, that I started a group of *concerned parents* with a petition for less homework. One parent mentioned the government slogan, "No Child Left Behind." This inspired me to alter the sentiment, and post signs around Piedmont that instead read:

"NO CHILD LEFT WITH TIME"

I was hoppin' mad that the girls had three to four hours of homework every night. It felt like there was no free time. I was determined to make time to bake together, go for walks with our dog Bagpipes, to see the Cookie Lady, make mosaics, plant bulbs, have "quiet time," paint floor-cloths, sing, sew quilts, build forts, plant vegetable gardens, take a ski-weekend, and just hang out. We squeezed in most of those activities; however, in general, I felt like the school system and divorce stole my children. "Family time" came last it seemed, as the pressure of homework and soccer was so extreme.

Claiming time with daughters;
Ski Bunnies: Jenny and Kate

The fact that I had only half custody of the girls did not help the situation. No one can fathom the physical and emotional division of the children that results from living in two households until it is upon you and them.

Because school demands and extracurricular activities were so overwhelming, every day after school, the girls and I would take one hour of "quiet time" alone, just to "be still." Each of us could relax in our own rooms.

I wanted desperately for the girls to have a well-balanced life and time to explore their "creative imagination." To have a balance between *academics, physical exercise, spiritual health, and emotional care*...like the 4 wheels on a car. If one wheel is flat the car drives poorly. And if all tires are pumped up, there is a smooth ride.

I was struggling as a single mom, fighting for the well being of my daughters and myself, and now a new and different challenge slapped me in the face. I was diagnosed with colon cancer and would need major abdominal surgery.

~Colon Cancer~

This first scare with cancer was in the summer of 2002, as my divorce was grinding to an end.

It all started when I noticed a dark red substance in the toilet. I tried to explain it away for months by telling myself, "Oh I ate beets last night" or "I had strawberry jam or red wine" or something else that would cause the dark red stains. It was hard for me to imagine that at forty-one years old, anything major was wrong with me.

When the stool test came back determining that it was in fact blood, I received a call from the "gastro doctor" who advised me with urgency to schedule a colonoscopy, "Right away."

A week later, I gulped down the horrible tasting gallon of saline water. My intestines were cleared out for sure after running to the bathroom nearly a dozen times during the night.

Doctor Goldberg was running a little behind, no pun intended, and once he arrived for the procedure, I greeted him with a little bouquet of sweet smelling flowers from my garden. Next I was ushered in for the colonoscopy. He asked if I wanted to be semi-conscious during the procedure, and I said "sure." I felt light headed and a bit dizzy as the IV meds kicked in. I gazed at the TV screen monitor as the snake-like probe was going through my colon and intestines.

All was going well until Dr. Goldberg said, "I need some help here Sandy," in a stern voice, and "I need to cut this out."

My heart skipped a beat as I saw on the screen a round, ugly, red- veined, marble-sized ball. Was this in my intestine? Was I dreaming? The slimy round face was smiling a sinister look at me.

It appeared angry, vengeful, and mocking. It was a devilish face. "Snip" and it was gone.

A few days later I got the results from the biopsy from the diagnostic colonoscopy, and sure enough it was evil. It was a cancerous, malignant polyp. The grape sized polyp was removed during the colonoscopy; however, I would need to schedule a major surgery to remove twelve inches of my lower intestine to make sure it was all out. The surgeon was concerned that the cancer may have spread beyond the colon wall.

~Grinding the Devil's Neck~

A few days before my next major surgical procedure, I was getting a sandwich at the Genoa Deli in downtown Oakland. There were no available tables to sit at, so I asked an older, rather large black lady with a purple hat if I could join her at her tiny round table.

She replied, "Sure honey, have a seat." I asked her how she was doing, and she asked me how I was doing. She seemed more concerned about me. Then I told her all about my colonoscopy and my next surgery coming up.

The sage lady looked at me with dark lavender eyes and said, "Honey the devil is trying to take you down. Now don't you let him, ya hear?"

"Oh," I agreed, "I guess I need to say get behind me, Satan, huh?"

Her eyes became huge, as she leaned super close to me and whispered sternly, "No! You need to grind Satan's neck under the heel of your shoe, you hear me?" She continued. "I said grind the neck of the devil under your shoe, the heel of your shoe, into the asphalt."

I looked down and saw her grinding her chubby worn heel into the grimy linoleum floor as I swallowed a bite of my Italian combo sandwich as a final splurge at my favorite deli.

I later found a Bible verse that says: *"And the God of peace will soon crush Satan under your feet."*

I knew that I would not be alone during my upcoming surgery. God was with me. He would crush Satan under the heel of my shoe! And this lady, like an angel, through her great faith helped give me the courage to get through it.

~Prayers and Surgery~

The day before surgery, my friends, relatives, and church family committed to praying for me right where they were at 4:30 p.m. — I lay on my bed alone at home at 4:29 in the afternoon and felt the heaviness of my tired body sink into the memory foam topper. A definition of disease: "dis" means "absence of" and "ease" means "peace or calm." I had physical and emotional ***dis-ease.*** A double whammy.

"Ohhhh," I moaned as I thought of the surgery, the colonoscopy, the divorce, my kids, and my life.

At 4:30 p.m. exactly, I felt the heaviness lift. I prayed to God, "Thank you God for all of my friends and family praying for me, thank you for overcoming the devil, thank you for healing me, I love you." Then it felt like my body was lifting off the bed, in the light of God's love. I was lifted high in His precious hand for a brief moment, as His faithful followers prayed for me.

The colon surgery was major surgery for sure. When I awoke from the colon resection operation my mom was there, and I was in excruciating pain. It was as if a train hit me in the stomach. As my mom tried to console me, she noticed that there was a "kink" in the little tube that was to deliver the pain meds in the IV in my arm, and nothing was going through it. She paged the nurse, and the kink was fixed. I was so glad I had Mom there as an advocate.

The twelve-inch section of intestines that had been removed was **cancer free!** God heard the prayers of the righteous, and He contained the cancer to the polyp that was previously removed during the colonoscopy. At that moment, I was just happy to be alive and thanked God that I would be around longer for my daughters.

The next day, a little humor started to return to my life. Before I could leave the hospital, they told me I needed to pass gas. How rude, I thought. My nurse, "Breezy" advised me to walk the halls to get things moving to pass gas. She had an appropriate name for this advice, I mused. I walked the halls of the hospital with my IV pole and thin blue gown for hours it seemed, but no gas.

Finally I called my mom in desperation and asked her to look in the girls' toy box and find the soft pink whoopee cushion that sounds like someone 'passing gas.' The next day when Dr. Goldberg was making his rounds, I had a nice surprise for him.

He asked if I had passed gas, and I smiled and said, "Yes, doctor, in fact I think I need to pass some more right now." My leg pressed down on the thick rubber balloon cushion, and I let it rip! The doctor's eyes got real wide, and my nurse, Breezy, raced and opened the window for fresh air. I had not let her in on my little joke. Everyone chuckled when I held up the whoopee cushion. My doctor let me go home a bit early based on my good humor, and "indomitable spirit."

Upon returning home, I felt like royalty, propped up in my queen bed with a canopy, as my dear friend Ocie answered the door and received flowers and delicious home cooked meals daily from our local church, my neighbors and friends. The meals would arrive at 4-5 p.m. every day for three weeks. These were scrumptious dinners such as chicken cacciatore, herb grilled salmon and summer veggies, cheese-potato-leek soup, spinach-walnut -cranberry salad, carnival quinoa, chocolate cake with mocha icing, fruit compote, and Chinese chicken salad.

After each dinner, Ocie would put the clean casserole dishes and bowls on the front porch for pick-up. As Ocie and I licked our chops at dinner one night she exclaimed "I could get used to this!" I laughed so hard that my gut ached and the stitches and staples pulled.

Powerful prayer and delicious food, two big perks of church life I thought.

Though my appetite came back, the recovery process was slow and painful. To this day I have a 6-inch incision starting at my belly button slicing downward. The fact that I was cancer free helped me move on with life. God had "crushed the devil under my feet," just as my deli friend Darla had told me. No follow-up treatment was necessary. I was glad for a new lease on life, and I knew I needed to make more changes, but old habits die hard.

~A Vivid Dream "Do Not Drink Wine"~

I had a vivid dream one night.

I saw, "DO NOT DRINK WINE!" in capital letters.

It was like a big banner. I bolted awake. I knew that God was talking to me. This was an important message, but do you think I listened? It was my lifestyle, all my friends drank, and I figured it was a "well-deserved escape" at the end of the day. I was overwhelmed with custody problems, finances, children, health issues, and I was lonely. Fetzer Chardonnay was my best friend come five O'clock. Alcohol temporarily numbed my sadness. And after all, I was not a "drunk" I reasoned. There was never a DUI. I never stumbled around the bar or slurred my words.

It was hard for me to admit that drinking probably had a strong hold on my life. My seventeen-year marriage had ended, and I realized for me, the root cause was anger and dishonesty. It was all fueled by alcohol.

So I lose a baby, my marriage, part of my colon, and have a vivid dream, "Do Not Drink Wine." Yet did I finally give up drinking? You guessed it: No.

~"Do Not Give Up"~

Over the next several years, the court battle and the struggles with my "ex" and his new wife wore me down. I sometimes felt like throwing in the towel, it was just too much. I felt that the world was trying to steal my daughters.

I fought for what I thought was right.

To top it off, an angry nickel sized mole on my arm turned out to be **melanoma**. Panic struck again.

Thankfully, it was removed and all margins were clear, but the added stress was tough. I seemed to always be in the *fight or flight* mode. Always waiting for the next shoe to drop...

The verse that I clung to during the several tumultuous years following my divorce was:

"Let us not grow weary in well doing, for in due time we will reap a harvest, if we do not give up."

The key words that helped me were: ***Do not give up!*** I had that verse posted all over my house, in every room and every translation of the Bible.

In December, I planted hundreds of tulip bulbs outside of our English home and they would remind me each spring of reaping a harvest as the bright colors burst forth. I was always amazed at how a dark brown ball could turn into a beautiful tulip or daffodil flower after such a tough winter. A miracle really. I had been through a "winter of cancer and divorce," but kept telling myself not to give up.

Gardening was therapeutic for me with the girls often helping, and we all made closer friends with our long-time neighbors in Piedmont. Our boxwood hedge was lined with colorful tulips, azaleas and hydrangeas.

In the midst of it all, I continued to pray for things to turn out well, and I wanted to keep growing myself. It was critical to endure through everything life was throwing at me, for my daughters and God. I wanted to become healthier in all areas: physically, spiritually, academically and emotionally. With that in mind, I enrolled in a Masters Program at Holy Names University in Oakland.

~A Masters from Holy Names~

I began the "Sophia Program" with great anticipation; Sophia means wisdom. My goal was for growth. The focus was on culture and spirituality. I felt challenged by the curriculum and for my Master's Project I focused on *children, relaxation and allowing time for creativity for our kids* and promoting these concepts in the community.

Exposing the truth about the morally bankrupt educational system in the affluent East Bay area was important to me. I was very upset that the schools were often teaching our children poor moral values and overloading our children with unnecessary homework.

One day my daughter came home from school and said they practiced saying *"F*** you!"* on stage in front of her drama class. Another time the drama students were required to do a monologue recounting a rape scene. The words started to haunt me because I helped my daughter memorize her lines, "up a notch, this B**ch can take a bit more." That is when I drew the line.

My dear friend, Margaret from my Lectio/Prayer group came with me to meet with the School Superintendent. We presented our concerns. The head of all Piedmont schools seemed rather unimpressed.

"Drama classes everywhere are employing new learning techniques these days," the Superintendent said smugly.

After more protest from us, she agreed to talk to the principal and teacher. Interestingly, the next year my daughter was not selected to be in the drama class, although she had performed so well in school plays.

I found out many schools no longer allowed PTA meetings. My own mom was president of the Parent Teacher Association when I was young. It was meant to keep parents involved in the education of their children. Now it felt like the school tried to keep us parents away, unless we were having a bake sale.

Competition, tests, perfectionism and loose morals were touted by the schools as the goal it seemed. Some of us parents noticed that the children were subtly being taught that family was unimportant, and that parents were intolerant and irrelevant. The implication was that the teachers were smarter and more important than parents. There were many excellent caring teachers. However even the greatest teachers often had their hands tied by the teaching requirements of the Department of Education.

There was extensive writing for my Masters program. To express the fire I felt for my daughters I wrote several poems. These are a couple of poems that I wrote:

Courage

Rage of the Heart!
"Cor" is heart,
Rage is rage!
I breathe fire like a dragon,
The fire flames from my heart to my tongue,
My children have been kidnapped by the Education Machine.
I scream in anguish.
What are we doing?
What are we doing to our young 'uns?
Who is in charge?
I'm stuck in cement, stuck in the system.
Ugh. My heart rages, smolders.

Ape

If I were an ape,
I would care for my babies.
I would feed them,
Cuddle them,
Stroke them,
Teach them how to thrive and survive.
I, yes, **I** would teach them.
What would I do if a group of apes tried to steal my babies?
I would scratch their eyes out,
I would shriek, scream, jump-up and down,
Hit and fight…slug.
Or would I flee?
No, I would fight.
I will fight.

****

Also as part of the Masters Project, I taught stretch and relaxation classes at the middle school and high school when Jennifer and Kate were students.

I received an envelope of thank you notes from the kids. One student wrote, "Thank you for teaching us to relax and stretch. It was the best part of my year."

I expressed my concerns in an article for the Piedmont Post, about the stress on our kids. Here is an excerpt from the Newspaper article I wrote:

OPINION: Starving for less Stress

According to a recent national study in the *New England Journal of Medicine*, 85% of children and teens state that they are overwhelmed. What is the source of this stress? Some say students have too much homework and too many demands on their time. There is evidence that over scheduling and unreasonable expectations lead to anxiety disorders, eating disorders and a myriad of other health problems.

I believe the source of this stress is due to the pressures from school demands, sports, or other extracurricular activities and the reach of modern media. The schools, media and entertainment world pressure our children to strive, consume and acquire in unrealistic proportions. Furthermore, kids' over-programmed lives leave them with very little left to control.

It is my hope that we can help provide an improved structure that encourages balance in our children's lives so that they have the time and space to grow emotionally and spiritually as well as academically and physically.

After posting the article, I sent boxes of "Stress Mints" to all of the High School teachers and encouraged them to relax and ease off on the homework. One day during this time I was inspired by the words of Mother Theresa. She once said, "We can do no great things, only small things with great love." It was in this spirit that I wrote the following simple poem:

Small Steps

I may not be able to do much,
But so help me God,
What I can do, I will do.
With fire in my heart,
Gritted teeth,
And a smile on my face.

Life was stressful and not always very enjoyable. As parents it felt like we were eating our kids alive. Weekdays were jam packed, and on the weekends there was more homework, soccer games, and church. Where was the time for a lemonade stand? Jennifer developed stomach-aches and often had a hard time sleeping. Kate developed shortness of breath. The doctor determined that these were all ailments as a result of the stress of school and homework, and of course the split of the family.

~Back to Pre-School~

In response to the poor morals from the head of Piedmont schools, I decided to get *back in the trenches* and try and make a difference. Armed with my Masters Degree and fire in my heart for children, I started at the beginning.

The pre-school my daughters had attended was looking for a science teacher. Within the week, I was back with the children, planting an organic vegetable garden, and drawing pictures of the new healthy food pyramid.

Singing the *A-B-C Song* while they washed hands, I said, "We have to wash all of those germs away!"

There would be a short science lesson each day. I explained to the children it was important to take good care of their bodies on the inside and out. "You need exercise, eating nutritious foods and learning to be peaceful."

Once a week we would do stretching where the children learned to pose as animals.

"I'm a big cat," one little girl said arching her back.

"Meooooow," the whole classroom echoed.

"Why are boys always cows," Jimmy chimed in. He always had the loudest "mooooo."

~Traumas, Dramas and Kittens at Home~

Church was a highlight for me and my daughters. When the girls were in elementary school, I taught their Sunday school class. My favorite Sunday was the day that all the kids washed each other's feet during Lent season. We had big plastic tubs with warm water, bubbles and lots of towels. I told them the story of how Jesus washed the feet of His disciples. One little boy, Kevin in particular, was not pleased as he had to wash the feet of a girl.

Years later, Kevin's mom came up to me and said that Kevin still talked about the washing of feet in Sunday school and how wonderful it was. Sometimes we just plant seeds and hope they grow.

When Jennifer was a junior and Kate was a sophomore at Piedmont High School, I found another way to connect with the girls and their friends. We started fostering kittens. We fostered several batches of adorable and tiny newborn kittens. It was so exciting, and the neighborhood kids and girls' friends came running over after school to bottle feed the fuzzy creatures.

"They are just cute little orphans," Katie said.

"We need to be their mommies," Jen chimed in.

It was the first thing on all of our minds when we woke up in the morning. The kittens sat in our laps as we cuddled and nurtured them, and they cuddled and nurtured us right back. When they jumped around the downstairs playroom it made us laugh hysterically.

We named all of the kittens and decided to keep Purrsy and Anabelle. We even fostered a tiny rescue dog named Mudbug, a scrappy ten year old pup that was scooped up from the Katrina Hurricane. He had been found in a shopping cart in front of the Superdome in New Orleans covered in mud. Quite a survivor.

It helped to find outlets like fostering pets, as I had a horrific time with the fall-out from the divorce. I felt crushed by the effects on my innocent daughters. They were often in the middle of arguments between the two households, and our daughters seemed to be the lightning rod for the family emotions.

It was anguish for me to have the girls under the influence of another household where values and choices were often different from mine. I did my best, but they were tough years for all of us. I was torn up inside. I watched helplessly as I perceived my daughters were in the middle of a horrible emotional and physical tug-of-war. I worried about older teenage step brothers and the lives of my young daughters. I noticed alcohol, jealousy, anger, and competition seeped into the lives of my children. I often wept at night.

Then I brought my concerns to "court appointed mediation," yet there was very little or no improvement. I realized that people are going to do what they want to do. I found that the courts don't seem to dig for truth and often have poor values as well. They don't know who or what to believe. I was falsely accused of locking my child in a bathroom for a "time out" and lost custody for two months.

"I've never seen a bathroom with a lock on the outside—sounds like you have been set-up," my attorney said.

The parents slug it out and the children are the helpless victims of divorce, with little input or recourse from the courts. I realized that there are so many interpretations of "What is in the best interest of the children?" Each divorcing parent thinks the "best interest" is for the child to live with them!

My precious daughters' stomach issues and chest pains from the stress of the ongoing situation lasted for years. In the middle of the night before 8th grade finals, the only thing that consoled my daughter was to hold her hand as we repeated, "God does not give us a spirit of fear, but one of strength, love and sound mind."

Things were never smooth between the households. At times Jennifer and Kate seemed to be the most "adult-like" in the situation of conflict between me, their dad, and their step-mom. The adults seemed like little fighting toddlers, including me.

One afternoon, I dropped the girls off at the "other" house and Kate left the back door of the SUV open by accident as I sat in the driver's seat. Their dad and step-mom approached that open car door and we started to argue. I think that I was 15 minutes late dropping them off, and was catching grief for it. I was so angry in that moment, that my foot pressed the accelerator all the way to the car floor, mid-conversation, and the car door closed with a loud *slam* as I sped away. I smiled with satisfaction at my swift maneuver that left them all stunned.

One counselor suggested we all suffered PTSD—post traumatic stress disorder, from a decade long custody battle.

"Do not grow weary of doing good," I reminded myself, "for in due time we will reap the harvest."

~Missions and Trips with Teen Daughters~

We did sandwich in a few awesome trips as the girls got older. The three of us made it back to my old stomping grounds in Michigan where they enjoyed eating corn on the cob and swimming in my favorite childhood lakes.

We went to Mexico on a church mission trip where we built homes for families who previously lived in cardboard shacks. It was a true eye opener for the three of us. Our showers came out of a plastic bag, warmed by the hot daily sun. Toilets that did not flush. We slept on the hard ground and developed a big heart for the faithful Mexican families that we worked with side by side.

Jennifer, Kate and I were in charge of the children and would play soccer with a ball that was deflated. We sang songs around the campfire each evening. We taught the kids arts and crafts, such as building little bird houses, making mosaic crosses, and water color painting. We taught them English Bible stories from a book that was in both languages. Each morning when our bus pulled up the dirt street to the worksite, a throng of children would come screaming and cheering to greet us. It was elating and humbling at the same time.

Our final day, one of the boys named Juan had a passionate spell while trying to hide his tears, as he realized that his "crush," our daughter Jennifer would be leaving for good.

I vowed to become more compassionate and less materialistic after this mission trip. For starters, I sold the rest of my fine jewelry. I longed for a simpler lifestyle at home, yet wanted to introduce my daughters to other cultures around the world.

Mission trip to Mexico with girls building homes

~Homeless Friends~

One other area that seemed to be a great outlet for us during all of the chaos of life during the girls' teen years was when we started to reach out to the homeless people in Oakland. I found that people living on the streets had a soft heart for hearing the Good News about Jesus and often encouraged me by sharing their life story.

One time I was traveling to Yosemite with my young daughters over spring break. It was during my traumatic divorce, so we needed a get-away. We stopped at a 7-11 for a snack stop. As we approached the store door, we noticed a man sitting, crouched over with a cup that read:

"Please Help"

I reached in my purse and dug out a few dollars and a Little Bible for him. I said sweetly, "You are a child of God."

I started to enter the store, and to my amazement, the small black man hopped up, danced a "jig" exclaiming,

"I know I am a child of God!"

His happy dance surprised me! My daughters giggled. Here I was trying to impart hope for this man, and he was the one dancing for God!

Another time, Jennifer, Kate and I were departing from our church after serving meals to homeless folks. There was a round woman with stringy hair and raggedy clothes standing outside the church. She asked meekly if I had any spare change. I looked into her pretty blue eyes, and empathized with her. I dug into my purse and found a twenty dollar bill and gave it to her.

Her eyes lit up, and she said, "Honey is there anything I can pray for you?"

I thought for a moment, and said, "Yes, continued good health." Then I asked what I could pray for her.

My blue eyed friend said, "Oh, I'd like to ride a llama, and I'd like to touch a buffalo, and I'd like to take African Ballet, and I'd like to learn to play the harp."

My jaw dropped. Here was this woman, living on the streets with such hope and aspirations. Where were my hopes and dreams? *Good health?* I thought. I was humbled.

Another time I was coming out of my exercise class in Oakland, and a woman was standing next to my car parking meter. I said hello, and then she politely asked for money. I gave her a few dollars and asked how she was doing.

My new found friend said, "I am doing good! I have been living on the streets for a long time and now I have an apartment, and am engaged!"

I smiled and said "God is good, isn't He?" She said yes, and she asked if I would like to pray with her.

I timidly said yes, and she put her hands on my shoulders and proceeded to sing a simple tune, "Thank you God, thank you

Jesus, thank you God, thank you Jesus…" over and over again for about ten or fifteen minutes. Our eyes were closed, and I felt as if I levitated off the ground after a while. I did not feel the sidewalk under my feet. I softly joined her, "Thank you God, thank you Jesus…"

I felt a strong calling to connect with my homeless brothers and sisters. Through their example I learned the definition of compassion means; "to suffer with."

~Building homes in Thailand~

One day, a friend at church mentioned that if we really wanted to help our homeless friends, we could join a mission group going to Thailand with Habitat for Humanity. We would be building two homes in one of the most impoverished areas near Lampang.

The next thing I knew I was on a flight that lasted twenty-two hours. Without time for recuperation, we arrived in a small poor village where a special toothless lady came running to greet me with a hug. Each morning she would run towards me with arms spread wide and just hold on. They treated us like movie stars and made us feel like our work and presence mattered. In fact the heart connection with the Thai families seemed more important than the cinder block houses we were building.

At a local school, I taught the children Bible stories and did art projects. I had brought one extra suitcase on the long journey filled with pastels and colored paper. Then the children drew pictures of the "loaves and fishes" Bible story we had shared. Fishes and food quickly multiplied on the children's art paper.

One darling Thai girl said something to me and smiled. Her teacher translated, "She said, 'I am getting so hungry drawing all this food!'"

Barriers with language and a Buddhist culture made it difficult to share my Christian faith. Smiles and hugs were my best strategy.

The following day our group went on a mission. Deep in the jungle, near the border of Myanmar, formerly Burma, we met the brave "Rangers for Jesus," who lived in a huge tree-fort. Wives and young children included. The rangers would cross the border from Thailand into Myanmar through dangerous territory to deliver medical supplies and Bibles to the natives who want to remain in small Villages, out of oppressive Government control.

Arriving back in Lampang, we visited some of the girls who had been rescued from sex-trafficking. Many of these victims of child prostitution and pornography now learned new trades, such as sewing, cooking and hair styling. We met with an undercover detective who investigated the houses of prostitution. So many girls were just children and young teens being held against their will. It was heartbreaking, but the recovering teen girls were thankful we purchased many treasures they lovingly made by hand.

Returning home was bittersweet. Instead of art supplies, I came home with a suitcase filled with handmade purses, silk dresses and woven scarves. All at rock bottom prices made by those sweet girls in recovery. The Thai people had endeared themselves to my heart. I would remember my little toothless friend for years to come. Her smile and hugs stayed with me.

~Healthy Birds Fly from the Nest~

There is a longing on the part of parents and children to have had their childhood lived in a perfect way. With the broken family, it can be difficult to forgive ourselves for our part in the dysfunction of the family. One of my Stephen Ministry Trainers told me that anyone with a pulse is from a dysfunctional family.

So I forgave my ex-husband and his second, now ex-wife for all that transpired during those traumatic years. I hoped they forgave me too. I apologized to Jennifer and Kate for all they had endured and any harm I may have caused. I am not sure what I would have done differently, maybe prayed more and talked less. I often went into "fight or flight" mode like a momma bear protecting her cubs.

I remembered my mom's famous quote, "Healthy Birds Fly from the Nest." And as the high school years were progressing, the girls started preparing for college. They got part time jobs and drove themselves to work. My favorite was watching their excitement for five mission trips ranging from Africa to Mexico. Attending church camps in summer helped them grow in faith and forge many close relationships. Jennifer and Kate were amazing through it all. It is hard for a mother to let go. Especially when there is such guilt from divorce. But I knew it was best for children to *fly on their own.*

My counselor, Carol, said, "You can't do their childhood over again, at this point—you did your best."

She said, "It is a very difficult time period when your children are 16-25 years old, as we struggle with letting them grow up and become independent. It is just as hard for the children to breakaway."

One friend described her letting go process to me, "Imagine that you are wrapping your child up in a beautiful gift box with a bow on top. Then picture yourself climbing up a graceful glass staircase with your precious box until you reach God. Then hand the cherished box to Him and thank God. Entrust your child to Jesus and God."

I began praying for my kids daily. I hoped they would remember the joyful days of childhood facing the future with hope. I wanted them to remember how much I love them. I also wanted to embrace the precious time before they left home.

~A Few Bad Bedfellows~

Several years after my divorce, I found myself, like many other new divorcees, thinking about remarriage. I longed for a mate. I did not know what God thought of remarriage, so I was digging for answers.

One friend told me, "When an unbelieving spouse leaves, or abandons the believer, they are not bound to the marriage relationship, but free to remarry." It was from 1 Corinthians 7:15, she said.

I also found a Bible reference that said it is better to stay single. I had prayed and journaled a lot about all of the divorce and remarriage stuff. I had repented of my mistakes and shortcomings in the marriage and divorce.

Then I tried finding a new mate right away, under my own power, not waiting on God's timing. This was hard on me and my teen daughters, as my focus became divided between the girls and my search for companionship. One famous psychologist cautions divorced parents to wait until the children are in college before dating or remarrying.

On the weeks I had my daughters I tried spending as much time with them as possible. However during my time alone, I became obsessed with finding a man to fill my lonely void. I became involved with a couple different men over the next few years.

These men in my life caused an instability and confusion for the girls. The good news is that I did not allow any men to spend time alone with my daughters, so there was no opportunity for sexual or verbal abuse.

I developed a relationship with an Episcopal "Priest." I was entranced and swept up by the fact that he was a minister and had such power and "wisdom."

He was not really all that wise; preaching that the Ten Commandments were not really Ten Commandments but "the Ten Suggestions!"

I was not too wise either. My guard was down due to always drinking wine together. So I convinced myself we would marry someday.

After just a couple of months together, we went on a long camping trip to the Emigrant Wilderness overlooking Emerald Bay. Our first night in the poorly pitched tent, I did it. I prematurely bonded with him. This is a nice way to say we had sex outside of marriage. This is what the Bible calls fornication, *ugh!* So desperate for love, that I gave myself to him. My new boyfriend the priest "had his cake and ate it too." And it wasn't a wedding cake. The following night was spent vomiting out the tent door. I had accidentally ingested mosquito repellent while eating nuts with my hands.

Several more red flags started to appear. As we became more serious, he was worried that I would "hold his feet to the fire;" especially regarding the truth of scripture. I had started to question some of his worldly teaching, that didn't go along with what the Bible clearly reveals.

He said, "People should live together before marriage." *How convenient*, I thought. He did not want to tell his congregation about me either. One time he had me "duck down" in the car, when we drove by his church! How hypocritical. His daughter slept with her boyfriend in his home and they smoked pot and he looked the other way. We were sleeping together occasionally, so I was a hypocrite too.

One afternoon, I showed him a verse about living together outside of marriage. Then I showed him a study that revealed a much higher divorce rate for those who live together first. A few months later, he broke up with me.

The break-up was devastating as I had given a part of myself to him. Maybe I was swayed by movies and TV shows that depict people casually sleeping together outside of marriage, and my longing to love and be loved. Deep down I needed to take responsibility for my behavior, but my fleshly desires overruled my conscience once again.

On the rebound, I met and became engaged to a man who was also not really walking with the Lord. He was "spiritual, but not religious." That is code-word for a "New-Age believer," or someone who often follows many different spiritual teachings like Hindu and Buddhism. In Ted's case he followed astrology, which should have been a big red flag.

My daughters did not like Ted, as they thought he was a "control freak." I mistakenly thought I was in love, again, and prematurely bonded with him too. *Slow learner.* Even as a faithful believer, I was blinded. We were not "equally yoked" as God tells us to be in our relationships. I later learned being *equally yoked* means that both people in relationship follow Jesus and His teachings. We are to be kind to unbelievers, but not make them counselors or spouses.

Things started to sour a bit just after the engagement ring was purchased on sale from Macy's.

~"Do Not Settle!"~

One night a few weeks after the engagement, I was home alone. I was watching **The 700 Club** on **TBN**, my favorite Christian TV show filled with powerful life stories and news from a faith-based perspective. At the end of the show, one of the hosts, Terry Meeuwsen said a prayer out loud to God and the viewing audience. She said something like;

"There is a Christian woman out there who is engaged to be married to a man who is 'spiritual,' but not a believer in Jesus.

God placed it on my heart to tell this woman: *DO NOT SETTLE!* If you are this woman listening today, I urge you, *do not settle!* God has a better plan for you..."

Then her crystal blue eyes opened wide and she looked right at me. I knew that God was speaking to me through Terry that memorable evening. I listened. I broke off our engagement and returned the ring. How do you thank someone on television for changing the course of your life? After that relationship I took a short break from men.

~A New Prayer~

Time marched on in the San Francisco Bay area for me. The girls were finishing high school. In the summer of 2007, seven years after the divorce, I prayed to God,

"Lord, I am so lonely, if you want me to remarry someday, please bring me a Christian, loving man, since I am not doing such a good job on my own. And if you want me to be single, please fill the hole in my heart. Oh, and please forgive me for my past..."

My good friend Karen had shown me some profiles and pictures of nice guys online on a Christian dating website. But I was adamant, I did not want to meet someone on a computer, I wanted it to be more spontaneous than that.

I had watched the Bachelorette show on TV and noticed that the bachelorette, Trista, chose the "nice guy," the poetry writing firefighter, not the naughty guy with slicked black hair. After that show, I decided that I wanted to have a nice guy too. But where would I find this perfect match?

One day a friend set me up on a blind date with a man named Roman. He seemed sweet on the surface. Then he mentioned being on the UC Regents Board of Directors. His cause was to get all Christian Creation ideas removed from text books. He wanted to prohibit home-schooled students from attending University of

California! Roman had bad breath, greasy hair and seemed rather impressed with himself. *Do not settle* I reminded myself.

~eHarmony Eric~

I wondered if there were any good guys out there, and thought about giving up. My friend Karen reminded me, "Hey, all you need is one good guy, why don't you try eHarmony since they match you up with people who have similar interests and values?"

Somewhat reluctantly, I filled out the long application, and joined the online dating site. And very soon I was hooked, checking the website almost daily for matches.

One month after my prayer to God and joining eHarmony, on September 1, 2007, an "Eric" from Elk Grove popped up on my computer screen. It said, "Eric is a match, and he would like to get to know you!" our profiles were almost identical.

Eric's profile said, I am passionate about:

1. My faith in God and Jesus
2. My sons and family
3. Creativity with music & Real Estate work
4. Dark chocolate

My profile said, I am passionate about:

1. Faith in God and Jesus
2. My 2 daughters & family
3. Creative projects and Interior design
4. Dark Chocolate

The things we loved and our values lined up exactly. *A match made in heaven!* And Eric from Elk Grove looked so handsome, but I was still in the S.F. Bay area and my girls were in the 11th and 12th grades. Furthermore, Map Quest revealed that Elk Grove was almost two hours away, so I contemplated deleting Eric from Elk Grove. In fact, Eric was one key stroke away from being deleted!

Thankfully, my dear friend, Frida said, "Oh Betsy give him a chance, he's so handsome, and likes God like you do." So I would give this guy a chance.

Eric and I communicated on eHarmony and on the phone for several weeks. We went through the four stages of communication with eHarmony.

There were the closed-ended multiple choice questions like, "What would you like to do on a free night with your partner?"

A) Go rollerblading or bowling.
B) Go out to dinner and a movie.
C) Watch the sunset and go for a picnic/walk.
D) Have dinner at home and talk by the fire.
E) Other (explain)

The second level was to choose from a list of "must haves" and "can't stands" in a partner. Some of my "must haves" were, "Honest, Christian, non-addictive personality, emotionally mature, kind, and willing to do counseling if needed."

The third level was to answer "open ended" questions such as, describe your spirituality, or what is your greatest fear? I liked Eric's answers and he seemed to like mine, and one September evening, Eric called me on the phone.

It was very exciting to hear his kind, energetic voice finally. We talked into the wee hours of the morning. I felt like a school girl. I could talk with him forever. Eric asked me on a date for September 22, 2007, in Walnut Creek for my birthday dinner and I accepted.

A few days later, I was driving to meet my eHarmony perfect match in Walnut Creek, "Eric from Elk Grove," and my heart was pounding. What would he be like in real life? Was he as handsome as his picture?

A little anxious, I called him from my car phone, "Oh, hi Eric, it's Betsy. I'm a bit nervous to meet you—and how will I recognize you?"

Eric sweetly responded, "Oh, we already know each other. After all the communication on eHarmony, no need to be nervous. And I'm wearing a black leather jacket."

My heart melted. *I already knew him.*

I drove my little red Mini Cooper with the checkerboard top to Walnut Creek. After I parked, I glanced across the street towards the restaurant, and saw the most handsome man in the world standing out front. He was in a black leather coat with his arms wide open to hug me. I ran across the street and fell into his embrace, and when I looked up into his sparkling blue eyes—

I knew this was the man I would marry.

We ate dinner at an outdoor cafe, and split the salmon dinner. When I came back to the table after going to the bathroom, I noticed that clever Eric had moved his chair around the round table to sit closer to me. Soon we were in his vintage white convertible looking for a place to dance together. After a fun evening of dinner, dancing, drinking and talking the night away, Eric gave me a ride back to my car. He even had a birthday present for me, a book and wooden bookmark.

As we said our goodbyes, he leaned over in the car and touched my cheek. The sweet kiss that followed sent a tingling throughout my body and my head was spinning with excitement and love. My gold-filled heart earring fell off into his car, like Cinderella's shoe. We giggled as we searched between the seats and finally found my gold heart shaped earring before our final goodbye hug.

After that first date, we spent hundreds of hours on the phone and email getting to know each other more. Every time we talked on the phone, my heart skipped, and my mood lifted. I was smitten.

God had blessed me with a kind, God-fearing man. He had answered my prayer. The courtship ensuing over the following year required travel between the Bay Area and Elk Grove. Sometimes we would meet halfway. The more time we spent together, the harder it was to leave each other. We were in love.

It wasn't all easy, as we had children and logistics to work out. We each had a closet full of baggage from past relationships that included not only clothes, but books, records, good and bad memories and family.

My future sister-in-laws gave me a beautiful bridal shower. I remembered begging my parents for a baby sister when I was little, and now I had three sisters; Nan, Christine and Jerolyn.

Eric and I did some premarital Christian-based counseling together, and we also dragged the kids to counseling. We were committed to putting God first.

In the midst of all the chaos and joy, Eric recorded a CD with original songs he wrote during our courtship. He would often "woo" me while singing songs from behind his grand piano at his "garden home" in Elk Grove. I would often slip next to him on the piano bench, with a glass of chardonnay, and sing along to Amazing Grace or Forever My Love.

~Married on the Bay~

We married a year later out on the San Francisco Bay on a fancy boat with sixty of our closest friends and family in attendance. Eric's older brother, Daniel, married us, in a heartfelt ceremony. Dan was going through chemotherapy for colon cancer at the time, but still delivered the most amazing message on love, respect, submission and a "three- twine cord." We would be "husband, wife, and God" woven together.

Exchanging vows with Eric on the San Francisco Bay!

Our wedding was a blessed event, where we read our personal poems and vows to each other. As the sun was setting behind Angel Island and the sailboats passed nearby, I looked deep into Eric's crystal blue eyes, rimmed with deep violet. When he read his handwritten vows to me, my heart melted into his:

"In giving all of myself to you,

I promise to pray with you continually.

Moving closer in mind, body, spirit and soul, rejoicing in our language of love.

Lifting each other upward, our hearts into one.

In giving ourselves to each other, we are now to become soul mates on a forever date.

Best friends, partners, lovers and holders of each other's hearts.

You are the brightest of lights to me.

Beauty is passing, but a woman who loves the Lord shall be praised. The heart of your husband will always trust you.

And I will always truly love you..."

Just Married

The Honeymooners

Part 2

Days of Deliverance

~Three Twine Cord~

After the sweet start, how was I to know that throughout the next several years, we would experience some of the best times together and yet some of the fiercest trials yet. Thankfully, God would always be in our midst fighting our battles with us.

We all hear the national divorce rate is fifty percent. Then I read a Gallop Poll revealing that married couples that pray together daily, have a 99% success rate. Only 1% divorce! I decided in that moment to pray with Eric every day. We often prayed for God to be the glue that would hold us together:

"Two are better than one...For if they fall, one will lift up his companion...if two lie down together, they will keep warm." (Ecclesiastes 4:9-11)

We would need to stay tight while remodeling homes.

~Flips & very few Flops!~

I have always enjoyed remodeling homes, staging and decorating "Fixer Uppers." Now I had, Eric, my perfect match to share my passion with. We could make a little money at the same time. After the real estate market crashed in 2009, Eric and I decided to create our own business together buying properties and remodeling them. We were combining Eric's real estate background, and my interior design experience. Several people mentioned we needed to have our own "Flip or Flop" TV reality show! We were buying fixer-upper homes, renovating and staging them with furniture. Then reselling for a profit, or renting them. Thankfully, we had more flips than flops. But one project involved the police...twice!

One of our largest endeavors in Elk Grove was a five bedroom three bath Mediterranean gut job. It was on one of the nicest streets in town, so no expense was spared—with our modest budget, of course.

~Remodeling Woes~

Over the summer, we used our favorite "Stan the Handyman" along with several family and friends to renovate our new Tuscan style "flip." We gutted the home, painted every room and installed hardwood flooring. Using our favorite technique for remodeling kitchens, on a budget, we painted the kitchen cabinets white and put on new fun knobs from Hobby Lobby. We also installed a few glass cabinet doors for a high-end effect. New stainless appliances and tin back-splash with silver faux "pressed tin" completed the face lift.

Our son, Grayson, helped shape the Tuscan Style grounds and planted a delicious organic garden behind the home. We even added a "Tiny Dollhouse Home" by converting a dilapidated 12'x12' storage shed out back.

When our Mediterranean Marvel was ready to sell, we staged the home with a blend of gorgeous antique and modern furnishings. Exhausted from weeks of hard work, we went to bed early one Friday night, preparing for our first Open House. The next morning we had a panic stricken call from our neighbor who was helping at the project.

"Someone is trying to rip off your new remodel!" Kathy said, jarring us awake. "All of the new appliances and furniture are stacked by the front door."

Frantically, we dressed and rushed across town to find out the fate of our latest "dream-home" remodel. *Our most perfect project to date*, I thought. *And now this...*

"Better call the police," Eric said, speeding along the Bradshaw back roads.

Arriving at the home, our neighbor, Kathy was waiting.

"There was a big truck with a trailer, getting ready to back into the driveway," Kathy said. "That's when I looked in the house, and saw everything stacked by the front door. Everything— right down to the pictures."

"The police are on their way," I replied.

"The truck and trailer pulled out fast and then circled around the block a few times glaring at me. It was a man and a woman," Kathy finished.

It sounded like a description of "Stan the Handyman's" truck and trailer, I thought. He had been our main handyman for quite some time. During the remodel, I had worried about him going through a bad divorce. He had come to the worksite smelling like pot a few times and had a wild new girl friend.

"Someone sawed off the lockbox," Eric informed the police. "But the lockbox was never opened, so I think they had a key."

We spent all day and night cleaning up the home and putting it back together. Once all of the appliances, furnishings, and artwork were back in place, we realized Stan the Handyman had not called or come to work that day, so Eric called him.

"We care about you, Stan," my husband said explaining the botched robbery. "We found your bolt cutters at the scene."

"Are you telling the police?" Stan asked demurely.

"We'll see," Eric said. We were pretty mad.

But later that week we decided to drop the issue completely. Stan had called and said, "I'm moving back to my mom's to try and get clean—I hope you can forgive me."

~Million Dollar Buyer!~

The next weekend at the Open House we were ecstatic when we received an "all cash" full price offer! The nice looking family said they had Thirteen Million Dollars from lottery winnings. We were happy to share in their great fortune. They immediately wrote a large deposit check. Before the Title Company could cash the check and confirm their winnings, the buyers called us.

"We wanna move in early," our buyer, Cliff, said. "Our Landlord is so mean—we plan to get out of our place and move in tomorrow."

"I'll call you right back, Cliff," Eric said, as another call came in. It was the Title Company.

"Just wanted to let you know the buyers check bounced!"

"Let's cancel the escrow then," my husband said.

The police were called once again. The officer explained, "These fake lottery scams are big these days."

We were duped. The family had even prayed in the home with us. Another realtor later told us a similar sounding family had stayed illegally in one of her listings for almost a year.

"It was impossible to evict them once they had possession," she said, "We never should have let them move in before the close of escrow."

That night, as we commiserated over our misfortunes, we made a decision to spend more time on Ministry work and less time on our real estate business. As a realtor, Eric could still sell a few properties on the side. And I could still do a little design work. We would trust God to take care of our needs financially.

"Hopefully this experience will not get us down," Eric said."Let's forgive and move on…"

That night we both read a fortune cookie quote,

Stay away from deceptive and negative people—they will create a problem for every solution. We had a healing laugh.

Three weeks later we sold the home at another Open House. A Kaiser doctor paid "almost full price."

"My children just love the tiny house in the backyard and I love that organic garden!" our sweet new buyer said. Later she invited us to a costume party to celebrate their new home and meet the neighbors. My faith in people was restored.

Remodel-Before   *Remodel After*

~Going Deeper~

Spending most days together, I realized that Eric was not afraid to do the deep work. Problems arose in our marriage, as they do in every marriage, and he pressed in looking at the difficult issues with me, and we did the deep work; often seeing a Christian counselor for advice. Some of Eric's best friends are ministers who gave us sound advice and kept us accountable.

In one afternoon meeting, Pastor Roger Babcock said, "Remember to put God first, then your marriage. The children, family members, friends and work come next." He continued: "What God has joined together, *let no man or child* throw under a bus!" Then a hush fell over the room and Roger whispered: "You must really treasure each other and your marriage—pray together often."

Eric was raised with lots of music and psychology in the home. In fact, Eric's Dad, Tom Soldahl, was a psychologist and man of deep faith, and Eric and his siblings were often guinea pigs for psychology tests from their dad. His family of six went to the Faith Lutheran church faithfully every Sunday.

The story goes that when Eric was just four years old, he came home from church one Sunday and hopped up on his Grandma's piano in Minnesota and played "*Jesus Loves me*," with two hands. We all have a calling in life, and Eric's gift and calling is to share the Good News of Jesus through piano, guitar, music and writing. He had written many original Christian songs that I thought should be on the K-LOVE Christian radio stations. And little did I know at the time, I would soon be singing original praise music with my newfound mate.

~MMM Ministries~

Eric and I were so excited to be married and working as a team. In addition to our remodeling business, we started a new mission together to help people rejuvenate and reconnect with God. We named it MMM Ministries. It stood for Music, Christian Meditation and Movement. On our first outing, we organized a weekend retreat at the beautiful St. Columba Retreat center on the coast north of San Francisco for a dozen participants. We passed out invitation flyers at a charity event, and then contacted church members and friends to attend the retreat. We even had the M&M dark chocolate candies made up that were blue and green with our slogan: *"MMM Ministries."* We decided to make it a weekend without drinking as St. Columba did not allow alcohol anyway.

Before long, we were staying by the peaceful Pacific Ocean at St. Columba, an old Celtic style structure. The sacred old redwood retreat was nestled on a mountainside, with a beautiful Chapel, once attended by Prince Charles.

We spent the next several days praying, meditating on scriptures, singing and taking long walks together as a group. In the evenings there was stretching and singing and then praying some more. Some of the meals were eaten together in "reflective silence," contemplating the goodness of God and our blessings.

One afternoon we all took a hike overlooking the ocean and came to an area where monks had built the "Stations of the Cross." There were beautiful images of Jesus carved from redwood. They depicted the stages of Jesus' walk on the day of His death on the cross. Eric played his flute while we walked slowly along the 'Stations of the Cross' and quietly sang "How Great thou Art." It was an enchanting, memorable weekend. Eric and I were off and running. Eric's older Mom attended and sang, stretched and meditated on scripture alongside us. *What a trooper*, I thought.

Arriving back home, we would be facing a spiritual battle.

The prior summer, a sweet Asian friend, Kim, had taught us a prayer:

"Dear God, please cast any demons away from us, drown them in the deepest darkest ocean and pour the cleansing, loving blood of Jesus over us, Thank You! In the name of our Lord and Savior, Jesus Christ, Amen."

Kim said she prayed these words every day—it only takes a minute so "Why not pray it daily for protection?"

This prayer had become part of our prayer meditation routine every day for months, sometimes twice a day. I wasn't quite sure why we were praying that prayer, but Kim was a grounded reliable friend, and I figured that the prayer couldn't hurt.

~The Spirits of Sheldon Inn~

Right after the retreat, my new husband and I had dinner at the Sheldon Inn, an old carriage stop that had been turned into a restaurant. The historic building nestled in the country was close to Elk Grove where we lived. It was to become an epic night, but something strange was a foot. First, we had a bottle of Chardonnay, followed by a delicious dinner, and dessert. It was a very expensive and fancy gold rush era restaurant, yet people seemed to be yelling over each other while eating and drinking.

Our pushy waitress had been rude to us and seemed annoyed that we were sharing meals and kisses. When we stopped to look at the old wooden bar, the bartender mentioned that the restaurant had a "Gruff Ghost from the Gold Rush days."

Upon arriving home after dinner, I began to yell at my new husband for the first time since we were married. I really let him have it. Afterwards, I did not remember much of the conversation or why I was so angry, but I do remember thinking I was not myself.

The next day, Eric said I seemed like a different person before going to bed. I remember being very nasty and caustic, almost spitting blame and venom. Maybe I had too much to drink that night. Was there really a "spirit" a "ghost?" Then I read my Bible to try and figure out what may have happened to trigger my anger and rage. I read about "demons" or the fallen angels referred to in the Bible. I found out that Jesus spent one third of his ministry "casting out demons and healing the afflicted." Why is it today we can't even mention the word "demon" without someone looking at us like we are crazy, I wondered? Did all demons just leave the earth? Then a Bible verse jumped out at me like a double edged sword, *"Be sober and on guard, your enemy the devil (and his demons) prowl around like a roaring lion seeking someone to devour."* (1Peter 5:8)

Maybe that referred to me…

~FLOORED~

It had started out as any other day. I did a little gardening, worked on real estate and design projects, and spent some time with Eric. We then had a light dinner at home and watched a bit of TV before bed. Before going to sleep, I read in bed. The last sentence that I read was a line from Sue Bender's book, *Plain and Simple.*

She was in a spiritual battle with anxiety and the "demons that roared." She answered them: *"Stop this!"* Then I dozed off.

It had been only a few nights since we were back at home after the St. Columba retreat. We kept praying that prayer of deliverance that Kim had taught us.

I awoke at 3 a.m. with unbearable stomach pain. I hobbled downstairs to get a glass of warm milk. Reaching for the refrigerator door, the pain overtook me.

I called feebly but urgently to my husband, "Honey, I need you!"

Immediately, I clutched my stomach, dropped to the hardwood floor, and blacked out. ***Quite literally, I was floored.*** I slipped into an altered state where a spiritual warfare raged. I heard demonic type voices shrieking. The screaming in my head was relentless. I am convinced two demons were screeching at each other, hovering around my head. I heard teeth gnashing and hissing, even spitting.

"We must leave now!! She is not a good host for us!"

The shrill voices continued while noisy cymbals clanged in my ears, the demons seemed to be arguing, barking;

"She will become a warrior for God if we leave!"

"No!! We must go now!!"

"Stay!"

"Go!"

"Stay!"

"Go!"

The voices were oppressing me, hammering my head. It felt violent. There were flashing strobe lights. It seemed like what hell might be like, and it was right in my face.

"Ahhhh!!" I groaned in my spiraling wild mind. Then, finally, there was dead silence.

It was like the silence after a ravaging storm. I lay limp, almost lifeless.

Slowly my consciousness returned. The voices in my head were gone; I came back to my sweet husband, back to the world. I opened my eyes and wondered who I was and where I was.

Eric was cradling me on the floor, and he was praying fervently in a special prayer language that I had never heard before. Eric said later on, that he thought he was losing his new bride. My eyes had rolled back into my head and he had given me mouth-to-mouth resuscitation during the surreal episode.

As I lay like a large wet noodle in Eric's arms, I felt my body convulse one last time. I rolled over onto the floor and purged every last impurity out of my body. I vomited, cried huge cleansing tears, and peed. My nose dripped. I purged, and I purged good. Every orifice of my body spit out the devil and his evil demon henchmen.

My precious Eric cleaned me up, wiped off the floor, and carried me back to our bedroom. I felt vulnerable, soft, exhausted. My body was poured into bed, and I slept hard.

The next morning I awoke tender, tired, and with a softer heart. I felt like a newborn baby. And in that moment when my eyes opened, I knew I would not drink alcohol again.

Eric and I looked at each other with awe and a bit of confusion. We wanted to make sense of what had happened the night before. The only explanation that we came up with was that God heard our prayers and purged the demonic influences. This makes absolute sense as we had prayed the prayer to: *"cast away any demons from us, drown them in the deepest darkest ocean, and pour the healing loving blood of Jesus over us,"* for months.

Eric and I believed the Holy Spirit had done a mighty work as a response to our prayer.

You know, we are "born anew" once in Christ and there can be many other remarkable spiritual renewals in our lives, and this was one of them. The alcohol stronghold was removed and God delivered us.

Remember—I had lost a baby, a marriage, twelve inches of my intestines, and had a dream from God "Do not drink wine," but it would take me being sprawled out on the floor half dead to wake me up.

After my deliverance from drinking, Eric gave it up too. He said he wanted to give it up for God first and foremost, and support me as his wife.

"You're more important than drinking, Honey," Eric said.

We were a "three twine cord" together on this. Dramatically the desire for drinking was taken completely away from both of us. There was no more dry mouth, no more puffiness or headaches in the morning. Eric's chronic stomach pains subsided.

And as Eric says, "We never need a designated driver!"

I had placed wine before God. In my life, I had been drinking on and off for over 30 years; mostly on. *One definition of addiction is: Continuing a behavior even when it has bad consequences.*

Through the resuscitation and my vomiting, Eric believed his wine addiction was also purged out. Angels and demons battled for both of our souls that fateful night. God was true to form and beat out satan. Then Eric found a verse that said, *"You cannot drink the cup of the Lord and the cup of demons too."* (1 Corinthians 10:21)

After our dramatic night on the floor, Eric and I agreed to enjoy life to the fullest without drinking, taking a trip to Tahoe to celebrate.

Exploring the Lake Tahoe Area

~Breaking Generational Curses~

One day our friend Jessica came by our home in Elk Grove and invited us to a conference at their Church. Jessica, who is married to an evangelist minister from Kenya, told us that a

Christian home can be made into a sanctuary, free from addictions.

That morning she gave us a strong message. "Strongholds can become generational, my husband and I are determined that *it stops with us!*" Jessica further explained, "We will not allow drinking or smoking, cussing or rage in our home. Because of our family history we needed to take a stance on it all." She elaborated that her relatives had a difficult time with this at first but now respect their decision.

Then she flashed her broad white smile exclaiming, "We are making our home a sanctuary for God."

Eric and I were taken with this revelation and decided:

"It stops with us!"

We wanted our home to be a loving safe haven, a place where feelings can be openly expressed, where the truth is spoken, and alcohol, drugs, rage and gossip are left behind. We saw how much pain drinking had caused in our lives and decided that we wanted to offer friends and family a refuge free of destructive addictions. We soon found ourselves with many new friends whose lives centered around other fun activities besides drinking.

~New Calling and Opportunities~

After being *Floored,* my husband and I found it easier to share the Good News with others who are struggling. Together we found several ways to share our faith. We resumed handing out Little Bibles; tiny one inch by one inch red, white, or black Bibles with a key scripture or two from each book. We gave them out to folks on the street and those we worked with or talked to in stores or restaurants.

I learned to ask people, *"How is God working in your life these days?* People light up with the question and love to share the positive things that God is doing in their lives. I learned to share a bit of my testimony, struggles and blessings with people, hoping to encourage them on their journey and how Jesus loves them.

I realized that God brought Eric and I together to do special "errands" for His kingdom. God blessed our marriage with so many things; doing music, parenting five awesome kids, remodeling homes, sharing the Good News of Jesus, and most of all being best friends.

Whenever we have tough times my husband says, "Let's pray about this."

In fact, we confirmed the Gallup poll that reported: *Couples who pray together daily have less than a 1% divorce rate.* We began praying together in bed morning and night. That night we prayed for God to lead me to new meaningful work where I could put my education to use.

That next morning, I drove our son to Bradshaw Christian School in Elk Grove. Arriving at the school, I felt a strong pull to talk to the administrator about teaching again. The next thing I knew, I was in a circle of kindergartners teaching them to read.

At the end of my first reading session, one of the little girls asked me, "Mrs. Soldahl, do you know the fruits of the spirit?" Then she quickly rattled off: *"Love, Joy, Peace, Patience, Kindness, Goodness, Faithfulness, Gentleness, and Self-control."* Then right away, all of the children chimed in together: *"And against these there is no law!"*

My heart melted. *Who is teaching who?* I thought.

Arriving home that afternoon, I was excited to tell my husband about my day, "I see great hope for the future, Sweetie. I'm so happy to be teaching children again!"

~Created to Celebrate!~

That fall, Eric threw a surprise birthday party for me with all of my favorite foods, family, and friends. We played badminton and volleyball on the back lawn of our home. We told jokes, and I laughed so hard that night that I cried.

I shared my testimony of how I was floored on the hardwood kitchen floor where I now stood. You could hear a pin drop. We toasted with non-alcoholic champagne before enjoying my two favorite cakes from our local European bakery. Eric had surprised me with a few songs he sang from the piano, a red velvet cake, *and* a dark chocolate layer cake with mocha frosting. One cake had a Roman candle sparkler on top, and it lit up like the fourth of July. There was a beautiful necklace he gave me too.

As my brother in-law Steve danced around to the Beatles wearing a polka-dot party hat he said, "This is the most fun I have ever had at a party without drinking!"

~Vampire Teeth and Curfews~

Not everything was a party, though. I learned that blended families have huge challenges, or "opportunities," as we like to say. When our sons Grayson and Nolan were going through a strange teen phase and wanted to be "like vampires," they bought pointy ceramic "eye" teeth online with their own money. They wore the teeth a lot for fun, and when they smiled the corner canine teeth emerged.

One day when we were in Yosemite for a reunion with all of my family, we were preparing to go to lunch. Grayson and Nolan said they did not want to go. They wanted to explore the area instead. Both young teens looked at us, and the pointy vampire teeth appeared ominously. Their eyes became very wide.

Then I used my *Love and Logic* parenting techniques and said, "It's okay if you don't want to go to lunch with us... but don't look at us if you get hungry!"

Everyone giggled, as we imagined them chomping into our necks.

High school was particularly challenging as we tried to stay on the same page. We did go to several Christian counseling sessions with most of the children, and Eric and I saw a couple counselors ourselves. One of our favorite *Love and Logic* techniques we implemented was the alarm clock curfew. Jennifer and Kate were particularly social as high school teens and wanted to go to all of the parties in Piedmont it seemed. Getting home on time after a party was always a big ordeal and often caused problems. The technique we finally implemented goes like this:

Parent: "What time can you be home from the party tonight?"

Teen: "By 11:30"

Parent: "Okay, let's say midnight just to be safe. I will set this alarm clock for midnight and set it on this table in the hallway between our bedroom doors. When you get home, please turn off the alarm and go to bed."

Teen: "Okay."

Parent: "If the alarm goes off at midnight, then I will assume that there is problem, and I will need to call you. If I can't get through to you, I will call your friends to track you down and make sure everything is all right. If you are home by midnight as scheduled, and the alarm is turned off, we will keep sleeping. Then we can catch up in the morning—Sound fair?"

This worked like a charm, and I believe only once did they come home and turn the alarm off and go back out! There were lots of challenges and opportunities with four teenagers at once.

Once when we called the kids down for dinner, one son refused to come out of his room. He was glued to a video game. Suddenly he came out of his room and gave us both a sullen wild look, "I just want to kill someone!" he said.

The next morning we called our counselor, Bob, and made an appointment for all three of us. During the session when our son complained about limits on video games and cell phones our counselor said, "There is always military school if you don't like your parents' new rules around your tech time."

We loved our kids deeply and wanted the best for them. When things were tough, we reminded ourselves that God loves them more than we do. The prodigal son story in the Bible comforted us during several episodes in our lives when the children pulled away or walked away from faith.

A friend once told me, "If your kids can make you really sad, they have too much control over you." That made me think...

It helped to remember the great blessings in our lives with the five children; celebrating birthdays, graduations and holidays with extended family and friends. It was incredible to have my two precious daughters, Jennifer and Kate, and three awesome sons, Grayson, Nolan, and Paul.

Bradshaw Christian High – Golf team: Nolan and Grayson.

~A Walk with Son Paul~

One day, I was delivering flyers in our neighborhood with my step-son Paul who was ten at the time. We stopped at a neighbor's home along the way. Cassie and her husband were smoking in their garage with the door open. "Come in!" She said.

Cassie had beautiful rich chocolate colored skin, bluish-green, milky eyes, and long curly eyelashes. She sat on a chair wearing slippers with a red scarf tied around her head.

Above the workbench in the garage was a sexy picture of sassy Cassie in a red negligee; her husband wore a tuxedo next to a shiny red sports car. Miss Cassie was posed leaning on the hood.

Cassie looked right at Paul and said, "I hear you have bad night terrors and walk in your sleep, Paul. You know, that is just the devil trying to get you. If it happens again, call out: 'Help me, Jesus!' and He will help you. You call out 'I rebuke you, Satan, in the name of the Father, Son, and Holy Ghost.'"

Paul chimed in and said, "Holy Spirit." She motioned her dark-skinned hand in an arc around the top of Paul's head.

"And Paul, your heart is pure and you are handsome too—good lookin'! Oh, and Paul, God wants you to sing and have fun!"

Fun times with Paul, Eric and Mom-Flo on Lake Tahoe.

~A Hospitable Hospital Christmas~

On a cold December night in 2010, I went back in the hospital. It had been eight years since my first colon cancer surgery, where I lost twelve inches of my intestines. Why did I land in the hospital again? Was there something I still needed to learn? There was my divorce, loss of baby Stephanie, colon cancer, and recently the *"Floored"* experience in the middle of the night.

After four days straight of vomiting at home, we called my dad, the wise retired doctor, and he advised us to head right to the hospital because I had an "acute abdomen." Eric rushed me to the emergency room where tests revealed that I had "adhesions" or scar tissue, in my abdomen from my previous colon surgery.

The scar tissue that developed in the years following my first colon surgery had grown around some of my intestines like sticky yarn or spaghetti so food could not pass through. There was a tube inserted in through my nose down to my stomach to drain out the gastric fluids poisoning and flooding my body. The pain was excruciating.

After three days in the hospital, while preparing for surgery, I realized my life was on the line. Without the surgery I could not pass food and would eventually die, the doctor said.

I gave all the doctors, nurses, and my roommate tiny little red Bibles. *This is why I must be here at Christmas,* I thought. Eric had snuck dozens of little Bibles into the hospital for me and fresh underwear too.

On December 24th, I was scheduled for surgery. We had prayed earlier, and I was ready for the operation to remove scar tissue that was choking my intestines. But there was a possibility this was my last day on earth. I had met my nice surgeon, a young, petite, bright woman. I was aware of the risks of surgery and also knew that there was no other option if I wanted to live. I would need to battle for my life on the eve of Jesus' birthday.

There were also family and friends pleading with God to get me through and an entire church prayer chain of nearly two hundred people. In the surgery center, everything was stark white. White lights, white uniforms, white teeth, white machines, white sheets, white counters, floors, walls, ceiling. Yikes, this place felt so sterile, scary, and cold.

Then I remembered some powerful words that my Dad had told me as a little girl:

"Bets, nothing keeps you down for long...you're tough!"

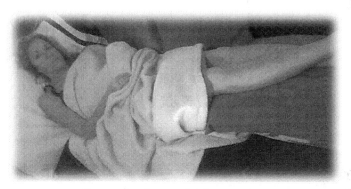

Recovering from multiple surgeries.

~An Operation on Christmas Eve~

In the surgery center, Eric kissed me gently on the lips, and then he was escorted to the waiting room. Then I prayed for the surgeons, I prayed for the nurses, and I thanked God for all of our blessings. Immediately my spirits were lifted, and the fear subsided. It helped that the IV drip anesthesia started kicking into high gear. Then everything went white...white, white, and whiter...

Three hours later, I woke up to my handsome husband's assuring blue eyes, as he held my hand. He lovingly told me that all went well and that I was okay. Oh, my gut hurt. I was up in my hospital room again, and Eric had quite a story to tell me.

~The Alarm Sounds at Midnight~

While I was in surgery, with my thirty-seven feet of intestines on the table, the surgeons had taken longer than expected. While they were painstakingly cutting off the numerous adhesions or scar tissue one at a time, Eric was in the waiting room.

Two hours into the surgery, the hospital fire alarm went off! The blaring alarm had sounded throughout the hospital for twenty minutes or so, as Eric raced around trying to get someone to turn it off. A man from the surgery waiting area had lit a cigarette. Was this the cause? Would they evacuate the entire hospital and leave me on the operating table? Uniformed employees raced around trying to figure out the problem. Finally, Eric found a maintenance worker and talked him into turning off the alarm without an evacuation during my surgery.

Eric pleaded, "If your wife was on the operating table, wouldn't you do everything in your power to make sure her surgery was safe?" The alarm was soon turned off. Eric breathed a sigh of relief.

"Thank you! God bless you Merry Gentlemen," Eric said while hugging the surprised custodians.

Then my surgeon had found Eric immediately after the surgery to reassure him all went well. The doctor said, "I heard that alarm going off, but I wasn't coming out of the operating room for anything!"

~A Christmas Recovery~

When I awoke from surgery it was Christmas day. My husband was in my room singing carols! Later, a vocal duo from church came to sing and elevate everyone's spirits. We joined in singing "Deck the Halls" and "Joy to the World" with several staff members and patients. I was happy to be alive on Jesus' Birthday.

Another bright note was that both of my daughters surprised me with a visit to the hospital as I recovered. They had been out in the working world living in the San Francisco area for some time now. We reflected back to their high-school years in Piedmont. Back then, I had taken each of my daughters on a separate trip to Europe, touring England, Italy, and France. I had sold an antique European tapestry and jewelry to help pay for our trips to Europe and our Mexico Mission trip.

I believe these experiences gave my daughters a longing for travel and to have a heart for the downtrodden. I was thankful that Jennifer and Kate were healthy adults, college graduates, and living or traveling abroad.

After the girls left, the drama continued back in my recovery room. My hospital roommate was a real character. Jane had legs swollen like telephone poles from thigh to ankle, due to "elephantitis," or severe edema or swelling. She moaned constantly. She screamed and yelled out when nurses touched her. But she also had a fun sense of humor and was surprisingly good company for me. She was diabetic and needed lots of shots and blood tests.

She often cried out to the nurses, "Please! I'm not a pin cushion! Ouch, Ouch, Ohhh!"

I would chime in, "Oh! God, please bless and protect my roommate, Jane. Keep her from pain!"

Jane would also intercede for me with heartfelt boisterous prayers, as the nurses stabbed my gut with a large three inch long needle, to keep the blood from clotting.

After Jane went home, I was assigned a new roommate at 2:00 a.m. the next morning, another moaner. This poor tiny lady broke her hip and was screaming in pain.

She screamed, "I want to die!" Then she started yelling obscenities at the nurses: "Just let me die…you X*%&%#!"

One aggressive nurse came in and told her, "You will go to hell if you die now!" It was clear; the nurse did not want this patient to die on her watch.

I called Eric at 3:00 a.m. crying because of all of the chaos and noise. I was trying to sleep and heal, and it was impossible.

Eric called the head nurse requesting a quieter room for me. Before changing rooms, I hobbled over to my room-mates bed with my IV pole in hand and shared how Jesus loves her, and that the nurse was wrong…

"You have a choice of going to heaven or hell," I whispered. "You can accept Jesus as your Lord and Savior and go to heaven."

I hope she heard the Good News through all of the commotion in our room. We can plant the seeds, but the Holy Spirit does the work. I read somewhere that we may be just one link in the chain of helping someone come to faith. Maybe I was at the hospital to share the gift of Jesus, right on His birthday.

The prophet Isaiah wrote,

"The spirit of the Lord is upon me, because the Lord has anointed me: he has sent me to bring good news to the oppressed, to bind up the brokenhearted, to proclaim liberty to the captives, and release prisoners." (Isaiah 61:1)

As a side note, I found out why my intestines flared up and became blocked and landed me in the hospital. **I was allergic to crab!** The flare up, combined with my scar tissue from earlier surgeries, were a lethal combination on my gut. In my research, I found that the top food allergies are: peanuts, tree nuts, shellfish, and dairy.

It would be paramount to stop eating *ALL* shellfish. *They are the bottom feeders of the ocean.*

~Standing on my Head~

One of the biggest blessings of my life is that I bounce back fast. Following my Christmas hospital stay, Eric and I found ourselves on stage at our beloved St. Peter's Church down the street. Our next door neighbors, the Senior Pastor, Richard Eddy and wife Karen were dear friends. Our church liked to have fun and every year tapped into the talents of its members at a pancake dinner. Eric and I came up with a silly skit.

Eric had the idea to dress up in baroque outfits for the church talent pageant. I dressed up in a cute German fraulein outfit while he played the long-lost grandson of the famous composer and pianist, "Johann Sebastian Bach." Eric pronounced it "back" in a funny German accent. In the little routine we worked out, my husband played the piano behind his "Bach" – while I scratched his "bach" – and made many "bach to bach" bad jokes. Then I proceeded to get the hiccups. Eric stopped playing the piano abruptly and fetched me a glass of water stating, "This cure works best if you stand on your head."

Next I flipped upside down on stage, standing on my head in front of the large crowd. Eric poured the water slowly into my upside down mouth. Defying gravity, I swallowed a few gulps to the astonished members of our church. Just a few weeks earlier they had been praying for me while on the operating table!

Eric and I were then asked to lead worship in another Sacramento area church, where everyone loved to sing along with hymns and modern worship music. We also helped with the music on Sunday nights at our local service down the street from us in

Elk Grove. With the pastor and his wife living right next door to us, the St. Peter's Church felt like home. Karen and I became buddies, while Eric and Pastor Rich would meet weekly for a morning prayer.

The months flew by as each week we looked forward to selecting the Sunday songs and hosting the worship team practice in our home. Even though things were going better, another big trial would occur at church. We would need to enlist the prayer chain once again.

~A Bloody Communion~

Easter came upon us, and now I was in the larger church sanctuary singing the "Easter Song," by Keith Green. After the song, Eric still played the piano while I waited in line for communion. Suddenly, I felt a gush of blood drop through my womb and trickle down the inside of my bare thigh.

I whispered under my breath, "Oh no, sweet Jesus—not again."

There were large bright red drops of blood on the polished concrete floor below me. Why did these things happen on my favorite holidays? Christmas and now Easter. *Good thing it's not carpet,* I thought as I glanced around the Greenhaven Church sanctuary. I grabbed my husband's navy jacket from the pew, tied it around my waist, and bee-hived to the bathroom. Tears streamed down my face as I sat on the toilet. Rivers of blood flowed into the water below me.

"Dear God, help me," I pleaded quietly.

Fist size clots of blood came out of me. It felt like pieces of me splashed into the water. Looked like raw liver. Gross.

"Help me, Jesus!" I cried softly, as I rifled through my purse and located a super plus tampon and a super-overnight maxi pad.

I took care of business; sat on the porcelain pot several extra minutes having a well deserved "pity party."

I took a deep breath and looked in the bathroom mirror making sure the navy jacket covered the bulls-eye red blood stain on the back of my silky, aqua dress. New "crow's feet" wrinkles seemed to have appeared between my teary bloodshot brown eyes. Eric's suit coat would need dry-cleaning for sure.

As I re-entered the side of the sanctuary, Eric smiled at me from the piano, while the choir sang "Amazing Grace." I forced a tired reassuring smile back at him and sat down in the last row of the church. He knew something was wrong. Communion was almost over. Two more songs and we would be heading home. I could get through it. I reached in the pocket of Eric's coat and felt a wadded up Kleenex. *Good job Honey*, I thought. I knew I could always count on him for an old Kleenex. My plan was to wipe up the blood stained church floor after the service, grab Eric, and get to the car and home pronto.

One sentence carried me through the Easter Service, *"Have mercy on me Lord, a sinner. Have mercy on me."*

~Pity Party~

Back at home the next morning after Easter Sunday, I started to reflect on my woes. *"Oh this is getting so old,"* my heart sighed as I recalled other times I had menstrual flooding emergencies, but never before in church.

The heavy bleeding had been ramping up over the past few months and even years. Some days I felt hopeless and wondered how I could carry on. I had already gone through two uterine surgeries to fix the problem but it was only worse.

As a fifty-year-old woman, wasn't I supposed to be having lighter, less frequent periods? As in "pre-menopause" or "menopause?" As the year progressed, I had more bleeding episodes and shorter breaks between my periods. It was as if my menstrual cycle was in reverse. I bled for three weeks, and then had a week break. The bleeding was getting heavier. I was getting weaker and my OB/GYN recommended going on a low dose birth control to regulate the bleeding.

So in desperation and against my better judgment, I went on the pill for three months. There was no improvement; in fact I felt worse. I was super bloated and gained ten pounds, so I went off the pill.

~Heavenly Wisdom~

Summer months were hot in Elk Grove, the central valley of California. Through it all we were teaching a *"Love and Logic"* parenting class at our home for other parents from our church. They say a teacher needs to "teach what we most need to learn." At the time, I needed wisdom for our teens. My problem was that I worried about them daily. Teaching the class helped me put things in perspective and was a productive break from the constant bleeding.

One evening I went for my usual walk around the block with our dog Bugsy. As I turned the corner, I smelled cigarette smoke. My neighbor, Cassie, was in her garage as always having a cigarette. She is the one that had predicted that our son Paul would be singing in the choir one day.

"Is that my friend Cassie?" I called out.

I walked up to her open garage and told her about my heavy bleeding and anemia. The two ablation surgeries where they scraped at the large grape-fruit sized benign fibroids in my uterus were not successful, I explained. Now I was bleeding more than ever. My neighbor noticed my anxiety was over a ten.

Cassie spoke volumes to me, "The devil has put fears and doubts in you. You need to go home and pray and find a Bible scripture. God isn't done with you yet. All this doubting has caused the bleeding to increase."

I shuffled the long walk home, while my Yorkie rescue dog, Mudbug, pulled at the leash and guided me into the bedroom like a seeing-eye dog.

Following Cassie's advice, I grabbed my leather bound Bible on my nightstand and it split open on its own to Philippians chapter one; "*He who has begun a good work in you, will complete it until the day of Jesus Christ.*" God had spoken to me. It was the verse I needed to keep going.

I had to believe that *God* would complete the good work he started in me. I could have faith that I was to heal. I was weary from being attacked with negative thoughts. Cassie was right about the devil. Suddenly, I screamed out these words in my bedroom, "Get behind me Satan—now!"

Later that night, I said a prayer with my husband; it was the prayer that helped deliver me from the demonic stronghold of alcohol earlier: "*Cast the demons away and drown them in the deepest pit, pouring the healing, loving blood of Jesus over us. Thank you, Lord.*"

~Fibroids~

That summer, one Bible story really helped me feel like I was not alone with my years of heavy bleeding:

And there was a woman who had a discharge of blood for twelve years, and who had suffered much under many physicians, and had spent all that she had, and was no better but rather grew worse. She said, "If I touch Jesus' garments, I will be made well." Immediately the flow of blood dried up, and she was healed of her disease.

Then Jesus said to her, "Daughter, your faith has made you well; go in peace." (Mark 5:25-29)

117

The verses helped, but old habits are hard to break. One afternoon, I was at home feeling depressed from heavy premenopausal bleeding. There was a knock at the door. It was a petite Asian woman who was a member of our church. Judy came bearing delicious food and angelic wisdom. She encouraged me to put my feet up and let my womb heal. She shared her experience of three surgeries in five months. Judy explained that she needed to ask for God's forgiveness for her doubts and fears during that period of her life.

Judy's eyes turned from brown to a soft emerald as she spoke of her surgeries and shortcomings and of God's love and forgiveness. That she needed to ask God to forgive her for her "stinking thinking" and turn a new leaf. Once she asked for forgiveness, things changed drastically for her. Through changing her thoughts, her health improved and her depression lifted.

Later, we ate the tasty BBQ chicken and salad Judy had prepared for our dinner. I contemplated my fears, lack of faith, and defeatist attitude. Cassie had told me the bad attitude came from the devil, and I needed to pray it off and read the Bible. Now sweet Judy had confirmed it.

I was tired, but knelt by my bed late that night, "Please forgive me Lord for doubts, fears, and for caving in to depression. Help me to do better."

I lay in bed and repeated the verse to replace the fear within me: *"He who has begun a good work in me will complete it until the day of Jesus Christ."*

Then with another deep breath, *"He who has begun a good work in me will complete it until the day of Jesus Christ."* Sigh, *"He who has begun..."* And finally sweet slumber. That night while I slept, I dreamed my God-given name was restored.

~From Betsy to Elizabeth~

A lamp lit up in my hand in this photo. Gave me great hope.
(not photo-shopped)

As I hit mid-life, God put it on my heart to change my name back to my birth name: Elizabeth. In the Bible there are several folks that God has changed their names, Saul to Paul, Sari to Sarah, to name a couple. It is usually done to show a remarkable conversion in the person's life. The conversions in my life seemed dramatic to me, so I was open to the change.

I really liked the name Elizabeth, and I felt a kinship with Elizabeth in the Bible who was Jesus' Aunt. After all, my parents had given me this name at birth, yet I never felt permission to use it. There was strong push-back from several people, but I stuck to my guns. I had been through too much to let other people tell me what to do at this point in my life. My counselor, Sue, said the definition of Elizabeth is: *"Dedicated, pledged or sanctified to God."* That meaning sealed the deal. No longer would I be *"Betsy Wetsy,"* the little girl in the flowered dress. I would now be Elizabeth Soldahl and embrace hope. Shedding another layer, I would claim my Biblical name. My growth would be paramount with more womanly trials ahead.

~Staring at a Lion~

We often found ourselves at the Elk Grove Vitamin Store for supplements and advice. One of my best encouragers was Olivia Angeli. I noticed that the word angel was in her name. She helped me find many natural vitamins and foods and also recommended her naturopath physician, Dr. Godby, and I noticed that the word God was in his name. *Two angels from heaven?*

Olivia did not mince words, "Your body looks frail and your skin is pale."

Then and there I decided to visit her doctor.

Doctor Godby was not smiling as Eric and I sat in his office a week later.

"Elizabeth, I just attended a funeral of a fifty-year-old woman." Dr. Godby continued, "I need to tell you that your blood work and lab results are **very** serious. You are severely anemic. That's the tip of the iceberg here," Godby said while explaining my tests. "There are some things we can do; however, you need to know that right now you are ***Staring at a lion right between the eyes.***"

"What do you mean?" Eric and I asked in unison.

Dr. Godby looked into my eyes with great concern, "You need to dig within yourself and instinctually find what you can do to survive this. Imagine you are in a jungle staring at a ferocious beast. Only you know the way to escape." I heard the urgency in his voice. "After reviewing your health questionnaire, it reveals you're a real perfectionist. —You will need to change the way you think."

Here was a third confirmation: *You will need to change the way you think.* It really struck me. After all, both Cassie and Judy had just told me the same thing.

Dr. Godby's wisdom flowed on. "With situations in life with children and family you may need to learn to be 'okay' with one of several outcomes, rather than needing things your way. You can't fix the world."

The voice of a previous counselor came to mind, *"Elizabeth, the Savior already came, and it wasn't you!"*

Dr. Godby pressed in, "You need to learn to trust God, to let go. Pray a lot, Elizabeth—pray a lot."

As we left his office in downtown Sacramento, he smiled warmly. We had a group-hug and Dr. Godby said, "God-be with you."

I forced a smile as I caught his clever play on words. "And also with you," I managed to say.

That next morning, it became more apparent to me that maybe a lot of my medical issues were not just in the physical, but there was a deeper spiritual battle going on. I began reading a devotional every morning before starting the day, followed with 20 minutes of silent meditative prayer. I resolved to be less of a perfectionist and live more in the moment, to replace daily worry with daily prayer.

Then, out of the blue, a friend called and asked me to join a "Moms in Prayer" group. I started attending. I was hoping that it would ease some of my stress by handing worries to God. Every Mom in the group selected one of their children to pray for with the group each week. We shared our burdens and pleaded for our children. This became a big part of my life. And not only was I less stressed about our kids, I started to see miracles and answered prayer in *their* lives.

Realizing my need to rely on God more, I prayed and talked to Him more often throughout the day. I read in my Spirit Filled Bible that He is a personal God who wants a relationship with us. I would need this lifeline.

~"She Could Bleed to Death"~

A week later I had another episode of flooding. I soaked five super tampons plus five maxi pads in five hours. Luckily, I was at home in our bedroom near the bathroom. At the time, Eric had been washing a lot of bloody sheets with bleach.

That night, I felt faint and dizzy. Eric phoned my Dad, a retired doctor.

He said, "Look this is serious stuff, you better get her into the doctor." When Eric asked him the worst case scenario, Dad stated, "She could bleed to death."

The *advice* nurse from the hospital called us back and Eric explained my situation to her. I rested on my bed, feet up with a large 24 inch square pee pad under my butt, soaked in blood. Immediately, I got on the phone when I heard the words, "emergency room."

I stubbornly asked the advice nurse, "What's so bad about all the bleeding?"

I did not want to go to the hospital; I had already endured two unsuccessful fibroid surgeries. *Eventually it will stop, right, and I will be post-menopausal?* My book on menopause said **aging** is *nature's cure for bleeding; with the tincture of time, bleeding painful fibroids dry up.*

Then I heard the nurse take a deep breath, "Well it could be fatal, you could bleed to death." This was the second time I had heard, "... *bleed to death.*"

~Pedal to the Metal~

"No—" I moaned softly as I sat up in bed at 1:00 a.m. and looked down at the Frisbee sized bright blood stain on my white sheets.

Eric whispered from a daze, "You okay honey?"

This is not good. I sat for a few minutes as my life-blood drained out once again. I noticed the skin on my hands and thighs were pasty white, sickly anemic. I crawled like a baby to our bathroom. Large red dots speckled the tile floor around me and large drips of blood stained my legs and feet. I pouted and a few tears slid down my cheeks.

Eric jumped out of bed now. This time he insisted we go to the E.R. after reminding me that the heavy bleeding had been going on sporadically for a few years.

"I feel faint and lost a few pints of blood, maybe quarts," I told him in a shaky voice.

Eric quickly grabbed my velour black sweater, black sweats, my purse, and some black clogs and helped me slip on the clothes. I wrapped a towel between my legs like a diaper and we hobbled to the car. Eric whispered with a coy smile that our bathroom looked like a "crime scene." It did. Blood splattered everywhere.

Eric asked, "Do we need an ambulance?"

"No – just pedal to the metal!" My seat was tilted all the way back, so I would not faint from blood loss, and my feet were on the dashboard as we raced on the back roads, arriving in record time to the hospital in South Sacramento. Eric ran to get a stretcher. I had to pee so bad!

My husband helped me to the bathroom and the hemorrhaging started again. This time even more blood poured out, "splash, splash." Suddenly, I dropped to the white tile floor in the hospital bathroom and passed out. **Floored again!**

Eric began yelling "Stat! Code Blue!" Again, my soulmate to the rescue.

"She needs a transfusion!" Eric had said.

Suddenly, there was a group of doctors and nurses crowding around me, scooping me off the white and now red tile, carrying me to the gurney. In a matter of minutes, I was hooked up to an IV, oxygen, and an "O positive" blood drip. *Okay—hang in there*, lying on the gurney, I cheered myself on.

~Embolization—A New Procedure~

At 2 p.m., only twelve hours since we arrived at the Emergency Room, I was floating into "La la land." A more recent procedure called a "Uterine Artery Embolization" was about to begin. The surgeons all agreed that a hysterectomy was a very last resort due to all of the scar tissue, or "adhesions" in my abdominal area. The risk of bowel injury was too great because the uterus was likely knit in place with strings of adhesions, some connecting to intestines. A sticky spaghetti mess inside of me!

My surgeon, Dr. Davis said he was starting to thread the flexible wire-like instrument into my groin artery at the crease at the top of my thigh. He would thread it through the artery that was leading to my uterus. Then he would place sticky "beads" in those arteries to stop the blood flow to the grapefruit sized benign fibroid growth in my uterus. Theoretically, this would stop blood to the fibroid, yet still allow enough blood to keep my uterus alive.

As I awoke from surgery, I heard the doctor say that he used two bottles of the beads and all went well. After regaining consciousness, I mumbled to him that the procedure was rather painless due to the IV meds.

In fact, putting the catheter in for peeing was the most painful part of the process. Ouch, that hurt.

Recuperation at home in bed for a week gave me time to write, read, and reflect. Finally, the bleeding was gone. I was spared and humbled.

~Painting, Digging, and Singing~

A few hobbies gave me sanity during those several years of menopausal woes in my life. One was painting china at the Painting Place with my mother-in-law, Florence. One surprise benefit of my marriage to Eric is that I gained another family. The Soldahl's have a large family.

The Soldahl Clan at Center Street.

That winter, after the procedure, Mother Florence and I painted Christmas plates, we also painted polka-dot mugs and Italian salad bowls.

We left our worries behind and concentrated on creating something beautiful and original, often as gifts for others. I appreciated Florence, as she sometimes let me recuperate at her peaceful condo in her retirement community in Elk Grove. She encouraged my writing and creativity while we attended a writing and art class together at her place.

Gardening was another form of therapy for me as I recovered physically. For years, my favorite gardening strategy has been to plant bulbs: Tulips, daffodils, hyacinth, amaryllis. My favorite day of the year besides Christmas and Easter is the day I wake up and the bulbs in the garden have sprouted!

~Feed Them and They Will Come~

During this period of health restoration, we were asked by our church to host a class on "The Truth Project." Every Tuesday evening we had a group of sixteen, or so, attending at our home in Elk Grove. I looked forward to the video lessons by Del Tackett from *Focus on the Family*. Scripture is shown to always be the ultimate source of truth. The word of God was shown to feed our souls. We would commence each class by singing a few songs around the piano and we always ended the class with yummy treats in the kitchen.

Eric says, "Feed them and they will come."

It is a challenge to make delicious desserts and treats with low sugar. It became a passion to create mouthwatering foods that are also good for our bodies. I began working on a book filled with recipes and healthy ideas for living. I planned to call it *God's Food*. These would include my scrumptious low-sugar Banana Bread and easy Fish Taco recipes. I tested them out on Eric and our Truth Project Group at our home. All of the gals wanted my recipes.

~Fred and Ginger~

While still recovering, the doctors encouraged me to start exercising again. One of my favorite remedies was dancing. Thankfully Eric likes to "rip a rug too." One night at his mom's retirement center, Camden Springs, we attended a special fifties show. We could not contain ourselves and jumped out of our seats after the first song. It took us a while to realize that we were the only ones dancing. In essence, we became part of the show.

The Elvis impersonator said, "Who is this good looking couple? Could it be Fred Astaire and Ginger Rogers?" referring to the old Hollywood dance team icons.

While Elvis Jr. sang the final strains of *"Blue Suede Shoes,"* Eric twirled me around, gently dipping me on every last note. The crowd sang its approval by their applause for us too.

For one full night I didn't think once about having any physical ailments.

The next week someone at church asked if we had moved to a retirement community. We were clueless when a friend in the grocery store wondered the same thing.

"Do we look that old?" we asked one another when leaving the store.

Then bending down, I picked up a discarded local newspaper. There we were in a big photo spread doing the twist. Me in a short skirt at the old folks' home. The headline read:

"Join the Seniors at Camden Springs for Lots of Fun!"

~I Believe Concerts~

Though I had suffered with challenging physical issues on the inside, my outlook was changing for the better. The prayers and recent operation worked. The intestines and uterine fibroids were all behaving. I was regaining my strength.

We would no longer be held back. Earlier, Eric and I had planned to put on several faith-based concerts together. I had never imagined myself singing in a concert or on a worship team. Now here I was ready to give it my all. In recent months Eric heard me singing in the shower and said he loved it. So I signed up for voice lessons with our church choir director. I wanted to improve and find confidence with my singing.

Eric asked, "Hey Hon, are you still up for doing a concert next month?"

Even though I was back dancing, he didn't want to push me after all I had been through.

After our first rehearsal, it dawned on me that the *"I Believe Concerts"* would be blessed. The Holy Spirit began working through Eric to coordinate a dozen musicians and singers on several original songs. There were also several sing-along songs in the line-up such as *"Amazing Grace"* and *"Love One Another Right Now."* I would share my testimony, play the tambourine, and join in singing.

Although I was not a seasoned singer, I was not afraid to be in front of people. My several years of cheerleading began paying off for the concerts.

One singer told me, **"Your audience is God."** This took the pressure off.

But we almost didn't make it to this concert at all. Just hours before the concert was to begin, Eric suffered a major gall bladder attack. Right before leaving for the church, he doubled over in severe pain. I kissed him and then ran straight to our two next door neighbors in Elk Grove for help. Both were pastors. Our good friend, Phil Fuller, was home and immediately came to pray for Eric. Then Phil sprinkled his forehead with anointing oil.

Suddenly Eric said, "Let's get to the church!"

The "I Believe" concert would go on as scheduled.

When the concert began, Eric was 100% there to direct the music from the piano, sing, and give his testimony too.

"The pain disappeared while singing. Those prayers were powerful!" Eric said later.

It seemed that Eric's whole family came.

When I shared my testimonial story, it was focused on love, healing, and forgiveness. I poured my heart out about the loss of Baby Stephanie. I shared that my sorrow, depression, and guilt had lasted for a year after losing the baby, how one Sunday during communion, the blood and bread became real. Jesus became real, and I received forgiveness by God's mercy and grace. I did nothing to earn it. Grace was a free gift from God.

During the concert that night, I revealed my life of huge contrasts; life threatening health issues, sobriety, new married bliss, musical concerts, children and parenting, remodels, great spiritual growth, and major surgeries. When I finished, a hush fell over the large crowd. At the moment of finishing my talk, I was at peace. In fact, we sang our signature song: *"Go In Peace."* At the time, there was no way for me to know more surgeries were to come.

The concert ended on a high note with everyone there holding hands and singing: *"Amazing Grace My Chains are Gone."* Mine were—*for the moment...*

~The Under-Wire Bra~

What do women do? We look at bras. Lots of them.

One day in a department store, a voice called out from behind the rack of bras, "Under-wire-bras can get you electrocuted, or they can give you cancer," a mysterious lady said. Then she disappeared behind the sea of bobbing bras. This petite Asian-American woman confirmed my hunch and then vanished. At the time, I did not realize this was a signal of what was to come.

"That's it," I whispered to my husband Eric. "I'll cut a slit and pull the wires out from all of my under-wire bras and buy a few new bras without the wires."

I enlisted my husband to walk around and squeeze the bras to see if they had wires or not. He's such a trooper.

I'm not so sure about the electrocution part, I thought, *but it stands to reason that the under-wire would cut off healthy blood circulation to the breasts and the milk ducts.*

Later when researching online, I discovered that underwire bras and antiperspirant both may cause breast issues.

~The Lump~

The lump appeared seemingly from nowhere. The previous month when I did my self-exam, there were no lumps, in fact I was so pleased that my breasts felt like soft butter, not fibrous, tough, and dense as in past years. I had cut back on caffeine, and so the pain in my breasts had disappeared too.

One night as I lay in bed I felt a lump. It was like a large marble. *Maybe it will go away on its own,* I thought. *Maybe it's just a fluid filled cyst or a fibroid that is benign.*

My mind raced...*Why God? Why have I had so many health issues, problems, and struggles? It seems like I've had more than my fair share. Are all of my ailments a result of my past poor lifestyle choices?*

The lump felt about a small inch in diameter. My breasts were rather petite and soft, more so as I'd gotten older, so the lump was easy to feel.

Eric said, "Maybe it's not that bad—it's rather small."

I was not quite as optimistic as I'd noticed that pesky left nipple looked increasingly different, slightly inverted and crusty, which was a bad sign according to my online search. To top it off, both of my breasts had felt sort of "tingly," or hot and prickly on and off for nine months.

Now guilt was setting in. There had been those many years of steady drinking due to stress. Ten years straight taking birth control pills. I now read that both can contribute to breast cancer risk. On top of that, there was my poor diet with tons of sugar, carbs and fatty foods. All combined it was a recipe for disaster.

~Cookie Cutter Biopsy~

The breast doctor carefully studied the letter that I handed her as I sat topless on the cushioned table in her examining room. I blushed as my sweet husband sat on a stool by my side.

Dear Kaiser Medical and Doctors,

This letter is to notify you that I take full responsibility for my health and decisions regarding my health care. I do not hold Kaiser Doctors or hospital responsible for my health or any outcomes.

I appreciate your recommendations and testing. My husband and I will prayerfully consider all of our options and let you know what medical plan we determine going forward. You are hereby released of any and all liability.

Sincerely, Elizabeth Soldahl

An article I had read haunted me. It indicated that the greatest amount of medical lawsuits are related to breast cancer. I did not want my doctor to feel obligated to recommend every medical treatment under the sun. I wanted her honest recommendation without fear of lawsuits. Looking at it spiritually, I wanted to keep God as my *Great Physician*. Both my dad and brother were doctors, and I had great respect and appreciation for medical practitioners. Yet, I did not want to place my doctors above God.

"I don't like the looks of this nipple," the petite Dr. De Young declared as her bright blue eyes stared intently at my left breast. "hmmm—this doesn't look right. Your nipple is somewhat inverted—a bit scabby and crusty." The doctor continued, "If you were my sister, I would recommend getting a biopsy right now."

Glancing over at Eric, I felt the skin on my chest heat up from nervousness. My chest was splotchy and red as I looked down. We all agreed that an immediate biopsy of the breast tissue was the way to go.

"It's just like a half inch round cookie cutter, I will numb you up with a couple of shots then press the round cookie cutter in to get a sample of tissue."

The doctor has such a sweet manner, I thought. *But this is going to hurt.* I lay back as the large needle pierced my nipple.

"Ouch!" Then I prayed softly out loud, "Lord Jesus have mercy on me, a sinner, Lord Jesus, have mercy on me, a sinner, *Lord Jesus, have mercy on me, a sinner, Lord Jesus, have mercy on me, a sinner...*" Finally it was over. The doctor said we should have the lab results in three to four days, and she would call me.

Later that day, a friend called to check on me: "*Fear not*, is in the Bible 365 times," she said. "One for each day of the year— remember to trust God, Elizabeth." Then we prayed together, but it was still hard waiting for those biopsy results.

~Big Needle Biopsies~

The lab results finally came back from my "cookie cutter" doctor, and next several needle biopsies were necessary. Then a *very stern* radiologist met me with a *huge* needle in her hand. She was not the type of doctor you want coming at your breasts with a six-inch needle!

The giant needle poked my breast and then *"Click!"* Every time the needle went in, flesh was snatched and pulled out. *Ouuuuuch!* I bit my tongue hard.

What is going on, Lord? Help me! I want to stick around and do more concerts, shake my tambourine, do some more remodels, travel with my dear husband, and watch our children get married. I want to paint with my grandchildren someday, read them stories, and tell them how Jesus loves them.

My tiny bruised breasts hurt so badly, and I felt so broken, so downtrodden. What next...

~Alarming Test Results~

At 8:06 a.m., February 12, 2014, my cell phone rang once again. It was sweet Dr. De Young, but a call that no one wants to receive.

"Hi Elizabeth, this is Dr. De Young. Do you have a few minutes? Is your husband there?"

"Yes," I responded, as my heart began to pound.

I lay down on the bedroom carpet with my feet up on the wall, waving Eric to my side.

"You might want to put me on speaker phone."

"Okay."

"I have news from the biopsies. I am sorry to have to tell you, it is invasive breast cancer. There are four tumor masses in the right breast and 3 in the left. This is not what we were hoping for. I'd like you to come in today for a mammogram and ultrasound, then we will make a plan for surgery."

Hearing that I had cancer, my body started shaking.

"Elizabeth, we are here for you. You can call me anytime. You have your faith and are a bright soul. I have goose bumps right now."

What a compassionate doctor, I thought. *She had goose bumps for me.*

I told her about the plans for our next concert, Lovestock, in June and asked a few questions about the next steps. After hanging up, I cried and cried on the floor. Then Eric kneeled down beside me. He held me tight and kissed my cheek. When there were no tears left, I breathed deeply, and in that moment realized that *I was not alone.* God was with me, and my husband was with me too.

I sat heavily on my soft bed and prayed as I began a new chapter in my life called breast cancer.

My friend Marsha responded to my breast cancer news with encouragement,

"Elizabeth, I am so sorry. I have been through this. You are a mighty woman of God. You are cast down by this news, but NOT broken. You need to sing in your home, in your shower, and recite scripture. And think of this—now you will have more testimony to share."

I did not sleep well after the painful biopsies and tough cancer news. There was a deep sadness and fear that I may be leaving my soul mate, Eric. We were having such fun with our music, Eric's original songs, and our creative renovation projects. To top it off, the veterinarian called a few days later, and our beloved Yorkshire terrier had cancer too…

~Mudbug's Last Goodbye...~

Remember the Hurricane Katrina rescue dog from New Orleans we adopted when fostering the kittens? Our feisty terrier had been with us now for almost a decade. Mudbug or "Bugsy" was now eighteen years old and very ill with cancer—just like me at the time.

I learned that rescue dogs have a very special connection and allegiance to their owners. I had once been featured with Mudbug in a television documentary on Katrina rescue animals. The "premier" of the documentary in the Bay Area had been on our second date, Eric reminded me.

It was SO heartbreaking to let go of this little pet. We will remember him chasing the large geese around the lake nearby on our walks in Elk Grove. The Sunday after Bugsy died, we heard that our pets would likely be in heaven when we arrive there. Our pastor mentioned that animals even know their Creator.

"It's in the Bible," Pastor Rich said, chapter twelve in Job. *All creatures know that God's hand made them.*

Bugsy taught us to never give up; to persevere through everything. Even how to survive in a hurricane! He always reminded me to cuddle up when things got rough.

We buried him in our beautiful rose garden out back in Elk Grove. He was resting peacefully in his curled-up seahorse position. After we buried him, Eric said a sweet prayer for our beloved pet. A week after we buried our little Yorkshire terrier, we were notified "Bugsy" made headlines through the veterinarians' website.

Best Buddy Bugsy – Hurricane Katrina Survivor.

Pet of the Year: "Hello! My name is Mudbug, I am the oldest dog in the Hatton Veterinary practice! Do I have a story to share with you! I originally lived in New Orleans, Louisiana, but became separated from my owners after Hurricane Katrina. I was found in a shopping cart outside the Super Dome, absolutely covered in mud with my big ears popping up. Hence the name 'Mudbug.' which means "Crawdad" in Louisiana Cajun slang. Anyhow, "Hop Along Rescue" took me in. I was very sick weighing only three pound, plus I had heartworms. They put me on an IV drip and sent me across the country to California. My very caring new owners adopted me several years ago and have loved me ever since. If you love the story of my rescue, like my picture!"

~Why Me?~

One restless night, I scoured the book of Job looking for answers. I wanted desperately to understand why so many difficult things had happened in my life.

In the story of Job in the Bible, Job, pronounced with a long "o," struggled with God. Job wanted to know why he had so many losses, sorrows, and afflictions. Job lost just about everything, his sheep, his oxen, his camels, servants, sons, and daughters. I thought I had problems…

When Job's body was covered with boils, his wife even told him to "curse God and die," but he hung in there.

The one thing he did not lose was his faith. At the end of the story, Job begs to know why so many bad things happened to him. Basically, Job is told, 'I am God, and you are Job. You are a human. Who are *you* to question Me?'

It was not for Job to comprehend exactly why things happen the way they do. God has a greater plan in place that we cannot see.

God knows all things. Things that the devil means for evil, God can use for good. My take home message that night was; it was not for me to question God. He knows best.

My responsibility is to trust Him. My job is to be content, whatever the circumstances. I remembered my friend Marsha's words, *trials give more testimony to share.*

As I digested Job's plight, I whimpered softly through my tears, *"I am yours Lord, save me."*

Eric rolled over and said, "It's okay Sweetie."

Then I crawled out of bed and lay on the floor face down, arms spread wide like an upside down snow angel and cried out, *"I am yours Lord, save me! I am yours Lord, Saaaave me!"*

My husband got out bed and knelt down beside me. Often he would just remain quiet and rub my back at times like this.

~Sue's Wise Counsel~

One day I would feel confident and strong with faith and the next I was a wreck. The highs and lows were too much to handle, so I made an appointment with my Christian counselor.

That Thursday, Sue was full of wisdom. She helped me correct some of my **wrong thinking** about my breast cancer situation. The Bible says to seek Godly counsel, *"There is safety in a multitude of counselors."* (Proverbs 11:14)

First and foremost, she reminded me that we need to remember we are *nothing* without the Lord, that *ALL things are possible* with God. At the start of each counseling session, we said prayers asking for the Holy Spirit to be present and to guide our meeting. That day was one *hour of power.* The notes I took say it all:

Me: "I feel like this cancer would have been caught earlier if I was more conscientious. I blew off the doctors."

Counselor Sue: "The devil wants to condemn and blame. We live in a sinful world, and sin brings disease to the world. God wants us healthy and whole. The enemy says, 'you are a bad person.' *The enemy is a liar. In fact he hates everyone. The devil is blacker than black. He wants us all dead.* The truth is you made informed decisions with your breast health. What the devil intends for evil, the Lord will use for good. *God is love, and He promises to always be with us."*

Me: "I feel afraid of the pain, the surgeries, death, hard decisions, and the 'not knowing' what is going to happen to me."

Sue: "You have a choice, Elizabeth, to choose peace or choose fear during this journey."

Me: "I want to choose peace, but the fearful thoughts creep into my mind. How do I choose peace?"

Sue: "Just do it. It's like that commercial, just do it. Just choose peace. Refuse to entertain the lies of Satan. Speak the word of God. Say, 'Jesus Christ is my Lord and Savior, I stand on the word of God.' Say it out loud! **The enemy can't stand in the same room with Jesus, he will flee.**"

The counseling session ended with a prayer and a hug. Stepping out of her office, I felt a renewed spirit.

Later that night, at Sue's instruction, I read:

"Put on the whole armor of God that you may be able to stand against the wiles of the devil. For we do not wrestle against flesh and blood, but against principalities, against powers, against rulers of the darkness of this age." (Ephesians 6: 11-12)

~Just "Do It"~

So, the next day I decided, "To just do it!" In every room of our home, I posted notes and started speaking forth expectations of healing. I began to recite God's promises from the Bible out loud:

—*Your faith has made you well.*
—*Resist the devil and he will flee.*
—*My days of sickness and disease are over!*
—*God forgives my sins and heals my disease!*
—*By His stripes I am healed.*
—*I can do ALL things through Christ who strengthens me!*

It was hard for me to see other patients and friends around me suffering and even dying while going through chemotherapy and radiation treatments. One other verse that I clung to was:

A thousand may fall at my side, and ten thousand at my right hand, but it shall not come near me. (Psalms 91:7)

One night I wrote in my journal: **Dear God, You have delivered me from childhood sexual abuse, the loss of a baby, the anguish of divorce and custody issues, colon cancer, melanoma, alcohol addiction, bleeding fibroids, and blocked intestines, so surely You will deliver me now!**

~Get it out by the Root~

One week before surgery, I met with my *Moms in Prayer* group, Kimberly and Robynn. That day they would be spontaneously praying for me in my home as I lay on the sofa.

Kimberly began praying, "Oh Lord, we receive your healing for Elizabeth. We receive that the cancer is being removed by the root!" Her powerful words echoed:

"Removed by the root—Removed by the root!"

We listened to a Healing Praise CD with many Bible scriptures on Jesus' healing. Jesus never refused to heal anyone that came to Him asking for healing. Then we held hands in a circle and sang along with the CD, *Give thanks with a grateful heart—give thanks to the Holy One.* The Healing songs and verses played softly morning to night in our home.

That night I prayed aloud, "Oh Lord, I am receiving by faith that I am healed, but is surgery part of the healing?"

The next morning I awoke before sunrise and continued praying in bed: *"Help me, Lord! The doctors want me to do surgery, chemo, radiation, and hormonal replacement drugs. We need to let the surgeon know by Friday. The woman in the Bible with the bleeding issue spent all of her money on physicians and, 'Grew worse, not better.' Then she was healed by Jesus. Please, Lord, make it clear what you want me to do. Thank you, Lord, Amen."*

I remembered the bible verse, *"If you need wisdom, ask God, and he will give it to you liberally."* (James 1:5)

"TRUST ME" I heard God beckoning.

I would trust God. I thanked him for all my dear prayer partners:

Moms in Prayer Group ;Robynn, Jamelle, me and Kimberly.

~"I Will Heal You"~

Now I had one day left to notify the hospital if I wanted to cancel the scheduled double mastectomy surgery. I lay in bed next to my husband and heard a powerful message. It echoed through my heart and mind; I believed it was the spirit of God speaking to me:

"I will heal you though the surgery. I will heal you through the surgery."

I remember asking God, "Are you sure?" and the message reverberated through my whole being.

Then jumping out of bed, I woke Eric up suddenly.

"God is going to heal me through the surgery!" I exclaimed.

The next thing that happened seemed to confirm that surgery would cut out the cancerous tumors *by the root* and heal me.

Every morning, I prepared a glass of warm water with fresh lemon and apple cider vinegar to help fight the cancer, sometimes with organic honey too. This was a remedy I learned from a long-term cancer survivor that had refused conventional treatment. As I cut the lemon that morning, I noticed a half inch brownish-black ugly growth on the side of the lemon. With a razor sharp paring knife I sliced off that end of the lemon. The rest of the lemon was in pristine condition. Could that bad spot on the lemon be like the abnormal lumps in my breasts? Would the tumors be cut off as easily, leaving the rest of my body clean and free of the disease?

Then during my morning devotional, I read: "***For I will restore your health and heal your wounds says the Lord***" (Jeremiah 30:17)

~Breathe *"Faith"* ~

Our dear next-door neighbors Pastor Rich and Karen Eddy invited Eric and I for dinner a couple nights before my breast cancer surgery. They had a visitor staying with them from Ohio, Pastor Curtis Lyon. His wife had survived breast cancer several years before.

I will never forget what happened after we ate our delicious chicken dinner. With Pastor Curtis on guitar and Eric on piano, we began a spontaneous spirit filled worship together. Then, everyone laid hands upon me, praying for a successful surgery and healing. The Holy Spirit was ever present in that circle.

Pastor Curtis looked at me intently and said, "Dear Elizabeth, I pray *'faith'* over you. I pray that you have faith in God to get you through this. **Faith** that you will be healed. Breathe, Elizabeth— Breathe Faith. Faith, Faith, Faith, *Faaaaith.*"

Pretty soon I was breathing, *"Faith, Faith, Faith."* I believe I saw my breath as we stood in a circle, "Faith, Faith, Faith, Faith…" I was slowly starting to wash my brain and heart with *Faith.*

As my husband of deep faith and commitment cradled me in bed that night, I whispered, "Faith, Faith, Faith. I have Faith, Faith, Faith…"

The next morning I awoke and wanted to understand what the Holy Spirit had revealed to my heart the night before. I found in Hebrews 11:1 *"Now faith is the assurance of things hoped for—evidence of things not seen."* So what God promised in the Bible and what He revealed through the Holy Spirit, *I believed.* That was my leap of faith. *After all how many times did God speak to people in the Bible who had faith to seek after Him?*

~Double Mastectomy~

It was 6 a.m. at The South Sacramento Hospital as our pastor and his wife prayed for us. "Dear God, we pray for Elizabeth as she goes in for surgery. We pray for the doctors, nurses, and for peace. We pray for all of the cancer to be completely removed through this surgery." The next thing I remember was rolling on my gurney into the operating room.

When I awoke from the surgery, Eric was there by my side and he said, "I love you Sweetheart—it went really well."

Then Eric smiled and squeezed my hand. My numb body slowly came back to earth as I blinked my eyes. I smiled back at my husband, my hero, my best friend.

Looking around I noticed all the white. White walls, white curtains, white uniforms. I was reminded of my other times in this stark white hospital.

All at once I realized that I was alive. At the same time, I realized that I no longer had any breasts. In fact, where my breasts once were, there were huge bandages covering up five-inch long incisions. There were tubes filled with blood coming out of each side. The tubes were draining the extra blood under the skin so it would not build up and cause an infection or abscess.

Over the following days, I had a trio of help, my husband, friend Esther, and daughter, Jennifer. They all took turns squeezing and draining those tubes twice daily. It was gross and uncomfortable.

I hate to even tell you, but three days after surgery, my whole right side became infected. It was bright red under the skin. Immediately, we were returning to the hospital for a second major surgery under anesthesia. The surgeons cut me open again and carefully removed the bloody internal infection. More cutting, more stitches, more pain. Ugh...

~Post Operation~

Five days post operation my diary read:

"I am so tired my chest aches. But I am filled with joy. Even though the pathology report is not back yet, I know I am healed. I believe this with all my heart. I am relieved in the midst of the pain. God delivered me through surgery once again. He is faithful."

Next I was being pressured for further treatment. My friend who is a pharmaceutical consultant told me that chemotherapy is "bug poison" and will burn a hole in concrete if a drop spills. I trusted the message, *"I will heal you through the surgery."*

Healing naturally after surgery without chemotherapy and other recommended pharmaceuticals was what we chose. The decision **not to have breast implants** also seemed best for me. I do not judge anyone for doing chemo or getting breast implants. We all need to make our own choices. After researching breast reconstruction and implants, I learned that implants can hide future cancer. They also may become very hard from scar tissue and adhesions, like a hard ball. And they may need to be removed or replaced every ten years, as they can rupture or deflate.

Thankfully, Eric was in agreement with the decision to forego breast implants and pharmaceuticals. Eric said, "You have a sexy ice skaters or gymnasts body now – It works for me."

It helped that the Olympics were on TV at the time, so I was in vogue. Lightly padded bras were my new best friend. The hospital even gave me my first two for free.

~Trusting my Hubby~

As I was bedridden during the recovery process, I was unable to write the bills or manage the finances or the household. I was forced to trust my husband to balance the checkbook and get food on the table. To my great surprise, Eric handled everything. The cats were fed, the kids got to school on time, and the utilities were paid. Even the laundry was done—who cares if the whites were not separated!

Eric cleared debts and got us in a better financial situation. I learned that women do not need to be in control of everything. My shoulders began to feel less tight.

Then one day while recovering, I found a book on my shelf that I bought at a garage sale the prior year. *The Excellent Wife.* It was a big game changer for our marriage.

A woman is designed by God to be a helper, not the head of the house, I read. What a relief.

Eric and I were partners for sure, but the burden was no longer on me. He had stood in the gap in so many ways. The major burdens and stress that I was taking on before surgery were not really mine.

As a man, Eric was capable and designed to be the spiritual leader. It was freeing for me to be a helpmate and female partner, not the "boss" always putting my neck on the line. I began to have more time and energy for restoration. There was more time for joy and creativity. Our relationship deepened, and we seemed to get along better.

My husband had stood beside me through all these surgeries. He had accepted and loved me—scars and all. He had stepped up as a man with finances and family. I wanted to spread my arms wide and shout from the rooftops, "I love you Eric Soldahl!"

~Surgery Results~

Ten days after surgery, the call came from my Doctor.

Eric was at work, and I was home alone.

"Hello Elizabeth, we have good news! We removed seven malignant, invasive tumors. *All* surrounding tissue and *all* four lymph nodes taken out were free and clear of cancer."

All my cancer was gone. I began to choke up so much that I could not talk. Taking a short breath, I managed to say, "Thank you so much, doctor."

I truly believe I was healed through the surgery, as God had laid that on my heart before surgery. Hooray!!!

When I got off the phone I jumped up and down and screamed at the top of my lungs, shaking the loft floorboards:

"THANK YOU JESUS!!! THANK YOU JESUS!!!"

Then I dropped to the floor face down, spread eagle, and cried hysterically and screamed "Thank you Jesus!" over and over as the tears dropped into the speckled carpet under me, the same carpet that I lay flat on just two months before when I received the cancer diagnosis phone call.

This time I floored myself.

I worried the neighbors would think I was crazy or in a fight if they heard me, but I didn't care. Luckily no one called the cops. It is a day I will never forget. The medical community confirmed what I believe God had already revealed,

"I will heal you through the surgery."

Just two weeks earlier, I had breathed faith, faith, faith.

"Lord, You restored me to health and let me live." (Isaiah 38:16)

"Our God whom we serve is able to deliver us..." (Daniel 3:17)

"Lord my God, I called to you for help and you healed me." (Psalm 30:2)

I AM HEALED, and Over the Hump!

Not only was I healed from the dreaded cancer, but I was healed from my other maladies. The menstrual-fibroid bleeding had almost dried up completely. And since avoiding shellfish and starting fish oil and probiotics, my intestines were behaving.

Eric believes if women can make it through their mid-life menopausal years, there is "smooth sailing" afterwards. They will live long and healthy lives after enduring such suffering; In Romans 5:4, I read: *Hardship leads to endurance, endurance leads to character and character leads to hope...And our hope is in Jesus.*

~Flat Chest, Fresh Start~

My gratitude toward God was overflowing. I recommitted myself to getting my testimonial book finished. I wanted to tell everyone about how God came through for me.

More changes with diet were imperative if I wanted to live and keep sharing my faith.

A few weeks after the double mastectomy, my *Moms in Prayer* friend, Kimberly, called. "Hey Elizabeth, I just heard about the 'Ketogenic Diet' on the *700 Club*. On their TV show, they said how a diet of protein, vegetables, and healthy fats can starve cancer."

That night, I read cancer cells will not survive without carbohydrates and sugar feeding them. Then Eric and I watched a preacher on TV discussing all the benefits of fasting. There were blessings both physical and spiritual. I took it all seriously.

The next morning there was a knock at the door. Our friend, Emily, who sang with us at the *I Believe Concert*, was holding a plate of black bean brownies and numerous samples of essential oils. A few minutes later, I was breathing in healing frankincense and lavender oils.

"They seem so powerful," I said.

"Yes—they were used in the Bible days," Emily whispered.

When I applied them to my chest, the oils were soothing, and the mastectomy scars started disappearing.

I was grateful for so many family and friends coming along side me during this season. Through all these surgeries I had learned to accept help from others.

Before falling asleep one night I snuggled up to Eric and said, "It's been hard for me to be dependent on so many other people."

"I know Sweetie," Eric said, "You've always been such a giver, helper, pleaser type. It was your time to be on the receiving end."

With a clean bill of health, we were ready for a new musical chapter in our lives.

~Lovestock~

One of our miracles was following through on an outdoor concert we had scheduled prior to surgery.

"Let's join with a couple of churches to put on an outdoor summer concert," my musical husband had said. "Instead of 'Woodstock' let's call it 'Lovestock.'"

"You mean dress up like hippies and sing?" I said.

"Something like that, but let's use Gospel words to old sixties type songs."

The next day we called to reserve the Land Park Amphitheatre in the Capital City of California, Sacramento.

Over the next couple of weeks we rehearsed with our large worship team and passed out two thousand flyers. The brightly colored flyers, resembling the famous concert, went throughout Elk Grove and Sacramento. We had no idea how many would attend.

The day of the concert it was 104 degrees in the morning.

That afternoon, we had three hours of "boiling hot" music. Maybe our ministry "Faith on Fire" was born that day. We were thankful that anyone at all came out in the heat. It wasn't a huge turn-out, but the folks that came seemed to enjoy it, and most stayed for the whole thing. One highlight was when our son Nolan gave a short talk. At the time, he was on break after his first year at Simpson Christian University in Redding.

The noisy crowd stopped what they were doing in mid-sentence with Nolan's opening words:

"Daddy, Abba, Father-God" Nolan prayed. "We love you..."

Then I gave my testimony including how God delivered me through the double mastectomy surgery only months before.

My big moment came as I finished the ten-minute talk, "So, the glory goes to God for my healing. I am done with my drinking addiction, I am done with my depression, I am done with my sugar addiction, I'm done with cancer, and now I'm done with my talk!"

My husband later said it was the longest applause and laughter heard all day. Then Eric closed the Concert singing, *Taking it to the Streets* and told the crowd to spread the Good News.

Lovestock Concert

~Weekend Trips with Daughters~

After my recovery and concert, I reached out to my daughters to have a closer relationship with them. I found it was best to connect with them away from the day to day pressures, on a one on one basis. Since we lived far apart it was challenging.

"Hi Kate! I was hoping to do one of our mother-daughter weekend trips to Carmel. How is your schedule these days?"

"Oh, I am studying for big tests at work, but maybe a short weekend trip?"

Soon we would be walking on the Carmel Beach snapping pictures of the Pacific Ocean. Whether it was with Jennifer or Kate, we found fun restaurants to dine at. Sometimes we rode horses or got a pedicure. I would treat them to a bit of shopping, and often we would find an art store for a creative project.

Spending time at the beach together seemed like healing salve for any cracks in our relationship. I would cherish my daughters and our mini vacations together. I was grateful that they could put the past behind us and enjoy a new start. Forgiveness seemed to be a theme in my life.

Horsing around with Jennifer.

Carmel by the Sea with Kate on a Mom – Daughter Weekend.

~Final Layers of Forgiveness~

"You finally forgave your Mom, Sweetie," Eric said as we drove home from our trip to visit family in Santa Barbara.

"What do you mean?" I said, miffed.

"Well, you seem nicer to her, cut her more slack, and are not on top of her for every little thing."

The deeper layers of the onion were peeling off. My heart had shifted from blame to forgiveness. My mom is a sweetheart, and if I was in her shoes, I may have done the same thing. That's just the way it works. She did her best to protect me and keep me away from Gramps after I told her about his "touching me."

Forgiveness, I discovered, is so vital for physical and emotional health. There are different stages of healing and forgiveness. It seems to come off in layers. I forgave Mom, Dad, and Gramps in my "head" many years before;

But it took another layer of healing to peel the bitterness from my heart...

Through the process, I was learning to forgive myself. Somehow with abuse, often the victim feels guilty and responsible. It's really about receiving God's forgiveness.

After all, the reason Jesus died on the cross was so that we can be forgiven for our sins and move on with a fresh slate. *And since God forgives me for my shortcomings, I needed to forgive others for their mistakes and mess-ups too.* Release them from their offense.

My favorite duet that Eric and I sing at every opportunity is about Jesus' love and forgiveness.

The original song is called *"Go in Peace"* with these lyrics:

"Jesus met a woman at someone's home one night
She entered very quietly and waited out of sight
She then stood by the Savior, who was about to eat
The tears that trickled from her eyes
She used to wash His feet – He said:
'Go in Peace, your sins are forgiven,
Go in Peace, you've shown great love,
Go in Peace your faith has saved you,
Go in Peace and Love....'"

One day after singing this song at a sweet little church in Yerington, Nevada, I realized it was time to call my Mom.

~Phone Call to Mom~

"Hi Mom, its Elizabeth."

"Oh, Hi Elizabeth!"

"Hey Mom, I am finishing up my testimonial book, and there is something I wanted to talk to you about."

"Oh."

"I just wanted to let you know that in the book, I mention what happened with Gramps when I was little. The reason I am sharing my story is that I hope it helps other women, mothers and daughters who may have had similar situations."

My amazing mother responded with, "Oh, Bets, I am so glad that you are sharing that. I think it is so important that other people know about these things. You know, I think it may help other women too."

My heart leaped.

"I am so glad you understand and feel that way, Mom. It is also an opportunity for me to talk about forgiveness in the book."

"Oh yes! Did you include that letter that you sent me several years ago?"

"Oh yeah, the one where I let you know that I love you and forgive you for the whole Gramps situation? Yes, I included that."

"You know, Bets I think it was the biggest mistake in my life, not protecting you better with him. I still remember the day you told me about 'Gramps touching you where you go pee pee,' when you were a little girl at the cabin in Michigan." Mom paused, trying to put the right words together and then continued:

"I remember that night, sitting on the stairs outside the cabin and thinking what I wanted to say to Gramps. I wanted to say, 'Gramps, you leave my daughter alone!' I did my best to protect you after that. Bets, things were so different then. These things were not even talked about in those days. There was such family pressure. Gramps may have gone to prison—your grandmother was so proper. I was the daughter-in-law. Dad thought it may have caused you more of a scar if we made a huge deal of it."

Tears filled my eyes as I imagined my Mom grieving on the wooden cabin stairs as a young mother.

"Oh, Mom, that must have been so hard for you. You did your best. We all make mistakes. I drank lots of wine while I was pregnant with Baby Stephanie, then I lost her. I made mistakes with Jennifer and Kate too. I hope they can forgive me someday. *Just know that I forgive you Mom.* God works it all for good. He forgives us."

"Yes," Mom agreed. "I'm so proud of you."

After a short pause I finished, "You know Mom, I am able to talk about sexual abuse and forgiveness with my testimony. And after losing Baby Stephanie, I re-found my faith in Jesus. Because things worked out the way they did, I have a story to share. Since Jesus loves me and forgives me, I am able to forgive and love you and others. I'm so glad you're my Mom. I am so glad that you're okay with me sharing everything in the book. I love you, Mom."

"I love you too, Bets."

Forgiveness is a choice, not a feeling.
Forgiveness=Freedom

Sweet flowers and forgiveness with my mom – lookin' good at 82!

~Liquid Tears~

More healing tears sprung from my eyes as I hung up the phone. There was finally closure. With the help of God, I released my Mom, once and for all, and my Mom had released me. It had been nearly fifty years since I was that little girl with the flowered dress and Keds sneakers at North Lake in Michigan. *With forgiveness there was closure.* That night I prayed that mothers and daughters, parents and children everywhere can forgive each other and communicate about these things. Prayers were heard and soon there was forgiveness with others, as well.

One day after the girls were off to college, their ex-step mom called me out of the blue, and we had an amazing and healing talk. It was very cathartic to share together.

Finally, I determined to get this book out—seven years of toiling—seven years of walking through the wilderness, typing, thinking, creating, fretting, writing, rewriting, editing, guilting myself, pacing the floors, not writing, and writing again. My nightstand drawers were overflowing with journals and notes.

Then there was another great surprise. I found a letter my mom had sent to her church friends many years earlier;

Dear Companions in Christ,

Thank you for praying for Betsy during this past week when she had surgery for colon cancer...she said she felt the energy of people praying for her. She had an inspiring faith through the surgery and waiting period.

The surgeon removed 12 inches of her colon after having removed the malignant polyp weeks before. The results are in and the pathology report says;

"No cancer in the specimen, no trace of it, nodes and liver are clear." I went to the Chapel at Alta Bates and said a prayer of thanks, then Bob phoned, and I explained this miracle for our daughter. He said to me, "It is unbelievable to receive this report! All of those friends praying must have energized the antibodies to eradicate the bad cells!"

God heard all of our prayers! With gratitude,

Mary Ellen Logan

I poured over this letter. Once again tears fell when it struck me that not only was God always with me and for me, but my parents had been in my corner too. They wanted what was best for me.

"Lord, how many times shall I forgive my brother who sins against me, Up to seven times?" Peter asked.

Jesus answered: "Not seven times, but up to seventy times seven!" That is 490 times! (Matthew 18:22)

~Double for your Trouble~

Right after reading Mom's letter, I studied the book of Job again. I was reminded that he was a faithful servant of God. The Lord allowed the devil to harm him, but not kill him. Job was struck down with such calamity and sorrow, losing his children, land, livestock, and finally his health.

The devil wants to "steal, kill, and destroy us," I read, but he can't do anything without God allowing it. And if God does allow bad things to happen, there is always a reason. It may be about getting our attention so that we can change our unhealthy habits or for our spiritual growth. It may be for trust, patience, or even to show God's glory when He delivers us.

Sometimes our lives may feel like Job's. At one point in time, I looked at my life and said, "Why God?—I believe in you and have tried so hard. Yet, I have suffered so many different things."

At long last, I began to understand the concept that God is God and I am not. We don't always get to see the big picture. It was my "job" to just trust. To have faith in God.

The end of the Job story is my favorite part. The Lord restores Job's prosperity *after* he prayed for his friends and forgave them. The Lord doubled that which Job once possessed. God gives Job "double for his trouble." Double the livestock, double the land—double of everything.

Because Job did not give up and kept faith, God blessed him twice, and he lived a very long abundant life.

When we persist, endure, learn, and press on through the trials, God often rewards us. Sometimes these rewards are spiritual instead of tangible ones. This seemed to be true in our lives as we journeyed forward. My life blossomed as my husband and I found joy in our remodels, writing, music, travelling, grown children, friends, and family.

It was important for me to remember that even though the devil wants to steal, kill and, destroy, Jesus came so that we may have life, and have it abundantly!

"So the Lord blessed Job in the second half of his life even more than in the beginning." Job is blessed with a double portion of what he had. (Job 42:12)

Eric gave me a good laugh one night by saying, *"Double for your trouble, or better yet—triple for your nipple!"* I was glad we kept our sense of humor through all the trials.

After all my troubles I wanted to reconnect with family under more enjoyable circumstances. It was great timing that daughter Jennifer was having a birthday. Katie orchestrated a surprise party at a swanky restaurant overlooking the Bay in San Francisco. At the end of dinner we surprised everyone by announcing our move to the Lake Tahoe area.

Birthday in San Francisco with Eric, Nolan, Mom-Flo, Jennifer and Kate.

~A Move to Lake Tahoe~

After God's awesome healings for me, we felt called to move to the Sierra Nevada Mountains by Lake Tahoe. It would be bittersweet leaving church family, neighbors, and friends behind in Elk Grove. We had been doing worship music regularly at church too. Eric and I said goodbye with a big potluck party at our suburban home.

We moved to *The Lake* right in time for the snow and cross-country skiing. Here is the letter we sent out to those close to us.

Dear Friends and Family,

As some of you may already know, we will be relocating to South Lake Tahoe to a cozy condo with a little view of the lake. Hoping you will come and visit sometime. We will be able to spend a lot more time with our 14-year old son, Paul who was baptized during the summer in Lake Tahoe by our 19 year old son Nolan, who is currently studying at Simpson University to be a pastor. Our grown children Jennifer, Kate, and Grayson are all doing well too! Jennifer is

159

spreading her wings by taking a job in Australia. Kate graduated from Loyola and has job offers in San Francisco. Grayson is finishing up a semester at the University of Hawaii.

Regarding my health, it has been seven months since the double mastectomy surgery. We are believing and receiving complete healing from God. Thank you for all of the prayers. The four lymph nodes were all clear as was the surrounding tissue! All "bad" cells were removed through the surgery. I am doing my best to stay healthy with a clean diet, exercise, centering prayer, and rest. Eric and I have started the Keto-lifestyle, eating lots of healthy fats, protein and veggies, and minimal sugar and carbs.

We will truly miss all of our friends and neighbors in Elk Grove. It has been a wonderful place to live for the past several years.

Love always In Christ,
Eric and Elizabeth Soldahl

Paul's Baptism in chilly Lake Tahoe, performed by his brother, Nolan

With my sign in Tahoe at Christmas.

~Walking the Strip~

Shortly after arriving in Tahoe, Eric was asked to become the worship leader at a Bible based church. Each week people would attend from all over the globe. Our son Paul was hired to run the computer system during the church service, projecting the words for people to sing along.

I loved singing on the worship team and used my *fish shaped tambourine*. Eric encouraged me to sing solos and duets with him that fit my alto vocal range.

Tahoe was such a different experience than living in the Bay Area or Elk Grove suburbia. Tourists were everywhere. Summer was filled with swimming and boating. In winter there was skiing and snow hikes through the pristine forests. While nature was so pure, we found that there was a very dark underbelly in South Lake Tahoe.

The casino strip was filled with all-night gambling, drinking, drugs, and prostitution. According to our pastor there was even sex trafficking. A lot of the locals were lured into the activities, as the casino life was the center of town. Some of the church members worked at one of the casinos.

My local hairdresser called South Lake Tahoe "poverty with a view."

"Is everyone addicted to gambling?" I asked her.

"Or worse," she said.

Wanting to see for myself, I walked through each of the four large casinos. Everywhere I saw downcast faces. Most people sat alone feeding their clanging machines while sipping cheap booze out of plastic cups. My heart went out to them.

Later at home I had an idea. "Hey Honey, I am thinking about making a sign and walking through the casinos, passing out Little Bibles and tracts—what do you think?"

"Maybe you will be on the news." Eric responded. "What would your sign say?"

"How about, **Feeling Down, Try Jesus** or **Jesus Came for You!**"

Two days later Eric dropped me off in front of Harrah's Casino.

I walked up and down the boulevard with my large sign on a yardstick, wearing fuzzy boots and a Santa hat. It was almost Christmas, so I began passing out little red Bibles. "Here is a gift for you," I said while handing them out.

I found myself talking with alcoholics and drug addicts on the street who thanked me for the little Bibles.

"I will read this right now!" One homeless man said. I prayed with a toothless woman for her health and a safe place to live.

Once inside Harrah's Casino, I placed Bible scriptures below the slot machines where the money would usually come out. *This is really easy!* I thought.

Right then I felt a hard tap on my shoulder. Spinning around, my sign almost hit the man in uniform. It was a security guard.

"You are not allowed to be in here with that sign," he said. "Follow me."

As I stepped onto the sidewalk, I invited the security guard to our church. "My husband and I do the music there." I said.

"We'll see," he smiled.

The following Sunday, after we finished our last song, *10,000 Reasons,* Eric had a tap on *his* shoulder. It was the same security guard from Harrah's who had shown me the door. Overhearing their conversation, I walked over.

"I owe you an apology," the security guard said quietly, looking around the room. "It's just my job."

"No worries, it's great you're here today," I said.

"The next time you walk through the casino, I'll give you a little more time," the guard winked.

With our move to the mountains, we had hoped that the serene environment would lead to stress-free living. Here we were surrounded by towering pines, gorgeous nature, and wildlife. Then we discovered there were drug-dealing drunken neighbors twenty-four/seven.

One nearby neighbor pushed her son down a flight of stairs after spraying mace in his eyes! He sought refuge in our home with his six year old daughter. We called the police and later testified in court three different times.

"And we live in a nicer part of town," Eric said.

Our pastor lamented, "South Lake Tahoe is infested with demons. – It is a very dark place."

After Christmas, the cold weather set in. We were exhausted from our "Tahoe trials"–literally –so we jumped at the chance to do a little music at a Calvary Church in Maui, Hawaii. Thankfully we had saved our airline miles.

On the plane ride over, we composed a song, *"Victory is Yours."*

We felt called to spread the Good News through music, concerts, sharing our testimony, and worship services. We began to plan concerts in Maui, Chico, Castro Valley, Santa Barbara and even in Israel!

"Maybe we can call ourselves Musical Missionaries," my husband said. The following month we headed to the tropical Island of Maui. "Well someone has to be a missionary in Hawaii," Eric said with a smile.

Singing at Calvary Chapel on the Island of Maui.

~ Singing and Hiking in Hawaii ~

Arriving in Hawaii, we took the "Road to Hana." It is often referred to as *"Hana; the Journey not the destination."* One night, we stayed at the Wianapanapa cabins right on the ocean in Hana. The loud waves crashed right by our front deck. This was the exact spot by the black sand beach where our family had stayed years before. Over the years, when needing emotional renewal, I had envisioned myself lying on this warm black sand beach.

Early the next morning, we took the Hana Park hike towards the seven sacred pools and bamboo forest. Our goal was the 400-foot-high waterfall. Grayson, our son, who was attending University in Maui, joined us. Being quite the hiker, he led the way up the long and winding Pipiwai bamboo forest trail. This time back on the trail in Hana, I felt God was leading us into unknown territories. We were discussing more music and travel.

Then while traversing toward the tall ribbon of water, Eric and I felt so energized that we composed a new song, *"The Last Supper."*

These are the words we sang as we hiked:

It all comes down to the last supper,
When the sky catches fire and we're called to pray...
'Forgive me Lord for I am a sinner
I receive you Jesus in my heart today
I know you died for me and rose again
Only You can take all of my sins away.'
And it all comes down to the last supper
When the sky catches fire and we're all called home,
Like the very last meal, if we don't tell a brother
The Bread of Life is right behind that door!

Eric and Grayson at waterfalls

~Israel Is Real~

The following year, after worship at a Calvary Church in Maui, we were invited by Pastor David Courson to lead the music on a trip to Israel. We told Pastor David and his wife, Robin, that we had to think about it— for about a second!

Throughout that next year, we saved our pennies for the Holy Land tour. Then we put together music booklets for everyone on the upcoming trip. Early November, we packed my tambourine and Eric's guitar and headed to Israel. We met our tour group in Tel Aviv which consisted of over thirty fascinating people from around the world.

Singing in the Holy Land

Our tour guide, Yuval was particularly interesting as he was a "Jew for Jesus" or a *Messianic Jew* as they call it. His stories were colorful and informative, and we were all inspired by his faith and hope in *Yeshua* –Jesus.

One afternoon on the tour bus, I asked Yuval how he came to know Jesus as his Savior. He explained while in the states, he had a bad motorcycle accident in Los Angeles. Each day while recuperating in the hospital, a cousin came into the room and read from the Bible and prayed for him. "I am a Jew," Yuval would say.

"Finally, I realized Jesus was a great Jew. He was the Messiah all Jewish people had waited for." Yuval smiled.

After giving us this amazing testimony, our guide sang us a great song. Soon the tour bus rocked and swayed along the road as we belted out the song Yuval taught us:

"Pray for the Peace of Jerusalem!
Pray for the Peace of Jerusalem!
Pray for the Peace of Jerusalem!
In Jerusalem we Pray for Peace!
Shalu, Shalom, Shalu, Shalom, Shalu, Shalom,
In Jerusalem we Pray for Peace!!!"

We were like a bus load of kids heading for camp. After we calmed down a bit, our guide explained that "Shalu means "pray" and Shalom means "peace."

The food, sites, people, and music were all amazing. Bible stories came alive. One highlight was riding on a wooden boat on the Sea of Galilee, where we sang *Amazing Grace,* and Eric and I danced to Israeli music. This was the same Sea where Jesus walked on the water and calmed the storm.

I felt a kinship to Jesus as I waded in the Jordan River, the same water where the Lord was baptized and had baptized others. We *swam* in the Dead Sea, which is 38% salt, so we really just floated. I felt a part of the Israeli landscape rubbing the Dead Sea mud all over my body as I stood on the shore of the sea. I thought back to the time when Jesus had rubbed the mud on the blind man's eyes to give him sight. As I lay in the most therapeutic water known to man, every cell in my body relaxed and there was a sense of gratitude for my own past healing.

*Leading music then dancing on a
wooden boat – Sea of Galilee in Israel.*

Then we made the journey into Jerusalem. While praying at
the Western Wailing Wall, I broke down in tears, feeling the
power of the Holy Spirit. Millions of other travelers had stood at
the same wall pleading with Almighty God.

The following day, we toured the Holocaust Museum where
we saw and smelled thousands of charred shoes which were
retrieved from the gas-chamber ovens. Some of the blackened
leather shoes had straps with a button on the side and a very low
heel. Others were slip-ons, almost like leather ballerina shoes.

We heard horrific stories of how the Nazis carefully told the
Jews "you are going to the shower barracks for a treat, a nice
warm shower!" And when the joyful Jews got to the shower
rooms, the Nazis turned on the deadly gas instead of cleansing
water. I wept. I felt devastated for them, and I felt rage at the
Nazis; deep rage that I will never forget.

In contrast, we sang sweet songs at the Mount of Olives, and tip-toed through the tomb where Jesus was likely buried and rose again. We had communion there.

Our Faithful Tour Group in Israel

Each day our group met some locals and ate at some amazing restaurants in Israel. It was delicious fare. Every meal was a plethora of healthy, tasty foods, buffet style. Falafels are common in Israel, like tacos in America. There were dates, tahini, cucumber, tomatoes, hummus, eggplant, olives, lamb, and fish. The colorful salads kept us energized for our four sites per day tour. And the pastries were small, but beyond compare. All food was grown locally, and *nothing* came out of a box. No high-fructose corn syrup, no preservatives, low sugar, therefore low disease, low obesity. It was such fun trying new colorful foods that nourished our bodies and souls. I vowed to make more cucumber yogurt salads and hummus when I got home.

For the most part the landscape was desert-like; however, the oasis areas were lush like Hawaii. There were tall palm trees, rivers and waterfalls. The weather was mild and usually sunny. Eric and I traveled light with just one carry-on suitcase and one "personal bag-backpack." My daily "uniform" was khaki pants, black comfort sandals, and a top of purple, mauve, or blue. Our backpack was filled with snacks, water, pen, and paper. Inspired Travel, the tour company, covered all the expenses right down to the tips.

It was surprising how safe we felt in Israel. We read that it is safer in Israel than Chicago. Apparently there can be trouble on the borders, as there are twenty-two Muslim countries surrounding Israel, each hoping to claim Israel for their own. Yuval, our tour guide, told us that the Jews just want to live peacefully in Israel, their Promised Land, but they will fight hard if threatened. In fact, Israel is unique in that military service is compulsory for males and females.

It was explained by our guide that as Christian-Americans it is in our best interest to be supportive of Israel because the Bible says, "Israel is the Apple of God's Eye." The Israelites are God's chosen people and our guide, Yuval said, "anyone who comes against Israel will be cursed and anyone who stands by Israel will be blessed." (Genesis 12:3)

So we heard the call to support Israel and to pray for the peace of Jerusalem. Eric and I now consider ourselves to be **Christian ambassadors for Israel**, telling everyone we can about Israel and encouraging folks to save their money and visit the Holy Land.

~Tie a Yellow Ribbon~

The following summer, our son Nolan went on a mission trip to Kurdistan, Iraq, sponsored by Simpson University in Redding. When he arrived home Nolan shared great stories from his trip.

The next week he proposed to his college sweetheart, Amber, overlooking Lake Tahoe! I helped Nolan make dark chocolate with white lettering, *"Marry Me?"* Nolan wrapped the trees with yellow ribbons to lead Amber to a granite peak, with a stunning lake view. Then he popped the question:

"Marry me?"

We peeked from behind the trees snapping photos and thought of the Bachelor show on TV.

Nolan's romantic proposal to Amber

The following May, his Professor, Dr. Griffin, married them in the Apple Hill area of Northern California.

Wedding with extended family.

"A man shall leave his father and mother and be joined to his wife and the two shall become one flesh," were the words that resounded from the minister.

On that wedding night, I reminded my husband of my deep love for him, as we danced under the stars.

~Australia~

We followed up our journey to the Holy Land and the marriage celebration by heading to Australia. Our daughter, Jennifer had taken a rewarding job with Quest. She talked us into coming one day when we were in a Tahoe blizzard. While we were snowbound, she was walking around on a gorgeous beach showing us the sites of her Oceanside town via Skype on her computer. The warm sun and sand of Coogee Beach called us, and we immediately reserved flights with our stockpiled airline miles.

Soon Jennifer and I were floating in the warm salty waters down under. Ahhh...

The boat ride to the Zoo was an adventure in itself as we motored by the Sydney Opera House and sipped a delicious Ferry Cappuccino. We walked among the kangaroos, koalas, emu, and crocodiles. Jennifer was animated and elegant as our tour guide. Afterward, we wandered the cobblestone streets of old town Sydney. Years before they were inhabited by thousands of convicts shipped there from England.

Dinner that night was at the needle restaurant revolving high above Sydney, taller than the Space needle in Seattle. The circular buffet included cucumber salad, kale medley, seafood, and Caesar salad. They offered tantalizing desserts, including napoleons, éclairs, designer cookies, chocolate dipped strawberries, and gelato. I broke my *Sundays Only* treat policy and filled my dessert plate... twice.

We cringed as we tasted our once-in-a-lifetime kangaroo kabobs, emu, and alligator bites.

We were just strolling alongside these animals, we realized, and now we were eating them. Jennifer, a vegetarian since childhood, gave us the evil eye.

At a neighborhood church by our hotel, we shared our experience of Israel to the faithful Aussies. We also remembered to pass out "Little Bibles" to most everyone we met at hotels, restaurants, and shops.

No Jet Lag Pills were a Homeopathic remedy that helped ease the physical fatigue and may have softened the tug-on-my-heart as we flew away from Australia and my sweet Jennifer.

With daughter Jennifer in Australia &
Koala Bear in tree.

On our way home from down under, we stopped off in Maui and joined the worship team at First Baptist Church for the service. I shared my *one-minute testimony* of how the loss of my baby brought me back to Jesus. Then Eric and I sang *"Go in Peace"* to a hushed crowd.

That afternoon we enjoyed snorkeling with the large green Hana sea turtles. We wanted to put off the flight home to freezing Tahoe as long as possible.

~Tests Give us Testimonies~

Late November in Tahoe, leaves were falling from the quaking aspens, and a dust of white was on the pines. There we led music for a prayer retreat at the Zephyr Point Conference Center. All were encouraged to write ourselves a letter from God, speaking to our deepest place of emotional wounding. Mine went like this:

"Elizabeth, my dear child,

Have faith in me! Do not worry about tomorrow. I will take your burdens. Rest, praise me, and enjoy your days on earth with your dear husband. I give you life in abundance!...Go out Elizabeth, go out with your husband and tell others the Good News! Share your testimony! Tell them how I love them. I love you sweet Elizabeth...Go my precious child, go!" — "Ok God. Got it," I whispered.

Worship Music Leaders for Tahoe Prayer Conference.

~Deliverance from Strongholds~

While there was new found forgiveness and purpose in my life, I noticed some deep spiritual strongholds and mental attacks that still erratically dogged me down causing mood swings and anxiety. I wanted more freedom.

Then one day while at my favorite Mill Works Café, my friend Debbie, gave me the phone number of a powerful healing-deliverance minister in Oregon. He had been a well- known gospel singer and speaker for years. His name was Marion Knox.

"My faith was set on fire after one healing session with Mr. Knox," Debbie said. "And the session was for my friend. I just listened in." As Debbie spoke, I noticed she was radiant and her blue eyes smiled. She offered me another pearl of wisdom, "I realized that we are all born wounded and broken, that Jesus is the answer and our purpose on earth is to Glorify God…."

In my first phone conversation with Mr. Knox I asked him why I should trust him. Mr. Knox said, "My only motive in doing this work is to serve the Lord. I don't charge for it." There was a pause on my cell phone. "I've helped over 3,000 people now, with healing and deliverance."

After talking to his wife for more reassurance, I decided to share my whole life history with him. He listened with compassion, and asked many thoughtful questions.

Mr. Knox then said, "Elizabeth, I don't mean to offend you, but have you accepted Jesus Christ as the Lord and leader of your life?"

I was offended. "I thought so," I said. *Deep breath.* "Remember when I lost my Baby Stephanie and turned to God?"

Mr. Knox replied, "It seems like *you* are trying to be the leader of your life— not trusting *God* to be the leader of your life."

He was right. And it was causing me great stress and anxiety.

"Oh...you may be right." I whispered. I felt flushed.

"Elizabeth would you like to recommit your life to God, making *Him* the leader of your life right now?"

"Yes." I whispered through soft tears.

"Would you like to repeat this prayer after me?"

"Yes." I conceded.

Mr Knox spoke slowly in a clear voice, and I repeated every word:

"Thank you Lord for loving me. Forgive me for my past mistakes, and sins, and help me to turn away from them. I now ask You to be the Leader my life. I will trust You and follow You. Thank you. *In the name of my Lord and Savior, Jesus Christ. Amen.*" I was resolute. I would cast my burdens to the Lord.

Later, my husband said that I seemed much more at peace and compassionate almost immediately.

"You're sleeping like a baby." Eric said.

At Mr. Knox's recommendation, I began reading chunks of the Bible more often, and praying during the day, asking God for guidance and help.

~Hearts Being Healed Ministry~

One exciting moment came in the midst of my talks with Marion Knox. Eric and I were invited to sing a song at the Hearts Being Healed Conference in the Sierra Nevada Foothills. At these one-day retreats, women share their stories of pain and trials, and of restoration and healing. There was worship singing too.

We arrived Friday to meet the organizers and pray for the conference. At sunset we began walking the grounds to bless and dedicate the land and conference to God. The leaders proclaimed powerful prayers for protection.

The following morning there was worship singing, followed by revealing life stories from several women and a sweet surprise from the dozen men that were serving us. At lunch I gave my "one-minute testimony" about losing my baby Stephanie and coming back to Christ. Then Eric and I sang *"Go in Peace...your Sins are Forgiven."*

That afternoon after the conference, one young mother came up to me, "Your talk and song at lunch really hit me," she said through tears.

"I have five children and lost an unborn baby too—I was doing some heavy lifting at the time—and I still feel guilty."

Janet and I had a bond; we both lost precious babies during pregnancy. My heart went out to this petite woman. We held hands and I asked if I could pray for her over the miscarriage.

Right there in the hallway we prayed, "Dear God, thank you so much for Janet. Thank you for loving us and forgiving us both for anything we did wrong during our pregnancies. Thank you that our babies are in Heaven, and we will see them again someday. In Jesus' name, Amen." We hugged and cried. I encouraged her to stay in touch.

****

I now believe that whether we women suffer a miscarriage, stillborn baby, abortion or death of a child, we are wounded at the deepest place of our soul.

Later, a wise friend confirmed, that babies who die in the womb will go straight to Heaven, because they are under the age of accountability. *"Let the little ones come unto me."* Jesus says.

~Spiritual Tune Up~

After the Hearts Being Healed conference, Eric and I traveled to the Carolinas where we were able to share some music and testimony as Musical Missionaries. We also remodeled a vacation rental property there. It was a three-week whirlwind on the East Coast. We had even talked with the *700 Club* about going on their TV program after our new books and the recording of our songs were out.

But I became run down and suffered from a horrible bladder infection. During the airplane ride home to California, I had to ask the man next to me to get up four times so I could go to the bathroom. The pressure and sense of urgency with my bladder was constant, and I was drinking quarts of water to flush out the infection. The thoughts that consumed my mind were all negative. The Devil taunted me, *"you have bladder cancer Elizabeth. No, you have ovarian cancer that is pressing on your bladder, no you have uterine cancer— actually you have cancer throughout your body."*

I called Mr. Knox again when we got home and told him of my fears from the bladder infection. He listened carefully, talked things through, and then asked me, "Elizabeth, are you ready to be free of fear, cancer, and infection?"

"Yes I am."

"Okay, let's pray off this fear, cancer, and infection." He continued in his kind reassuring voice to command in the name and authority of our Lord and Savior Jesus Christ of Nazareth that all spirits of fear, cancer, and infection be cast into the pit of hell. He prayed with such authority, "Elizabeth, I pray that you will have a *long* healthy life and that you will be free of cancer, disease, and infection. I pray that you will have **excellent health** until the day the Lord takes you home to heaven."

I believed in the healing and words prayed over me. The next morning I woke up in our home with all bladder infection symptoms gone! And my fear of cancer was gone too. Eric and I agreed the following week that we hoped to live to 106 and 100 years old respectively, and that we will be super healthy until the end and die in each other's arms like in the movie, *The Notebook*. But we always want to be ready. Jesus could come back tomorrow.

"As a man thinketh in his heart, so is he." (Proverbs 23:7)

"If two of you agree about anything they ask, it will be done for them by my Father in heaven." Jesus.

"He (Jesus) gives orders to impure spirits and they obey him."

~Richard –The Sweetheart Senior~

When we travel as Musical Missionaries, we often find ourselves talking to strangers about faithful things.

One recent night while dining at the Baywood Retirement Center where Eric's Mom Florence lives, we were seated with a man named Richard. He was in his nineties and was new to the Baywood Community. After introductions, the conversation found its way to faith. Richard mentioned he grew up as a Catholic, but since WWII, had not believed. Eric mentioned his own Dad had been at the "Battle of the Bulge."

"I was in the Battle of the Bulge too!" Richard said.

My husband then related a story about his Dad hearing from God to "move his men" and narrowly escaping an attack.

"There are no atheists in foxholes," Eric continued.

"Except me," Richard replied.

Then Eric mentioned how the thief on the cross hung next to Jesus and accepted Jesus at the last minute.

Eric looked right at Richard, "You can repent and be forgiven right before you die, and get into Heaven."

By now, most of the elderly diners had left. I realized Richard had finished eating before we even sat down. He wanted companionship.

"Do you have any family?" I asked.

"No one."

My heart went out to this dear man. I leaned in, "Richard would you like to accept Jesus as your Lord and Savior right now?"

"Oh, yes I would." He said.

I placed my soft hand over his. Then trying to recall the *sinner's prayer*, I remembered the song Eric and I wrote in Maui. I whispered in his ear, "Would you like to repeat a prayer after me?"

"*Yes.*" He said.

I began the prayer and Richard faithfully repeated each line after me:

"Forgive me Lord, for I am a sinner,

I accept You Jesus in my heart today,

I know You died for me and rose again,

Only You can take all of my sins away,

Now I make You the Lord and leader of my life,

In the name of our Savior Jesus Christ, Amen."

When he opened his eyes he lit up with a big smile. Eric and I explained that he was born anew with the promise of going to Heaven through his faith in Jesus. "Do you have a Bible?" I asked. "We always encourage people to start a prayer life, read the Bible daily, and share your new faith," I finished.

When we were leaving, my husband paused, "I know we're going to meet again in Heaven, Richard."

"Yes!" he said sporting a large grin, *"This was the best dinner of my whole life!"*

~Singing in the Desert ~

The following morning, we said goodbye to Eric's mom and the senior center. We headed to Palm Desert and La Quinta, close to the border of Mexico. There we started recording a new CD of original songs at the FOSS Christian Recording Studios.

One day we took a walk at the Shields Date Gardens where there were wonderful gardens reminiscent of the Holy Land. It brought us right back to our visit to Israel. Now at Shields in the California desert, we discovered there were statues and scenes depicting the life of Jesus.

The following Sunday, we sang at church and told the story of "Richard the senior" who accepted Jesus at Mom's retirement community all by the grace of God.

After the service, we organized a large group from the church to go to brunch and take the Shields Date Garden walk with us. Along the way, we sang and read the scriptures on plaques that went along with the scenes, such as Jesus being baptized by John. Spontaneously, I waded into the small lake to join Jesus and John in the water. Our group stayed all day until the sun began to set. It seemed we all just wanted to stay in these Heavenly gardens with Jesus.

~A Chance to Share~

The next morning, I received news from a board member that I was accepted to be a speaker at the Hearts Being Healed Conference!

"You have been selected to be one of the speakers in Chico at our March event. We are looking forward to hearing your story," Laura said.

I was excited and honored to be a part of this awesome ministry of women whose purpose is to provide a safe place for God's Holy Spirit to heal and restore hearts. I had prayed that there would be opportunities to share my story, hoping to help others with similar struggles.

God was opening doors. Remember as a little girl my voice was silenced? Now I would have an opportunity to speak the truth from a place of love.

Things were coming full circle.

~One Last Walk in the Desert~

While finishing this book, there was one more powerful moment. Taking a writing break, I grabbed Eric for a cool night time walk in December. We were still in the Palm Desert area to lead a Christmas worship service.

"I didn't realize the desert could get so cold at night," I said. "I'm freeeezing!"

On the walk I glanced at the moonlit Santa Rosa Mountains and mentioned that I did not know how to end my book.

Eric said, "Remember that time when Pastor Curtis prayed with us before your surgery? Curtis spoke, *'faith, faith faith'*— maybe you need to finish up your story with something about that."

For a moment, I recalled that life changing event. "The Holy Spirit was powerful that night," I replied; "it's soooo cold," I grabbed Eric's arm tightly to cuddle up. Right then while walking, I whispered, *"faith, faith, faaaith."*

As the words left my mouth, a strong gust of *warm wind* enveloped us and my body felt a sense of calm. I stopped and looked at my husband. "Hon, did you feel that?"

"Yes!" my husband exclaimed.

The Holy Spirit was comforting me to press on...

I kneeled down right in the middle of the deserted street, and thought back to everything that God had delivered me from.

"Thank you God, thank you Jesus"...I began to weep.

Then, rising to my feet, we held each other tightly as a December star twinkled brightly overhead. At that very moment I remembered the words Jesus spoke to the woman, "Go in Peace, your *faith* has made you well."

And she smiles at the future ~Proverbs 31:25

Traveling Musical Missionaries

Singing and Sharing Testimony

BONUS

Lessons, Remedies and Recipes

Lessons

Body image and weight:

Motivation and habits are the key to many things in life. With music, I have learned that motivation to memorize a song, coupled with repeating the song over and over is the secret. With weight and body image it seems similar principles apply.

There has been a struggle with weight and body image ever since my Grandfather told me, "You look so plump in that swimsuit."

Most of us have eating and binging struggles and I am no exception. The following are a few of my secrets:

- **_Motivation:_** Why be trim and healthy? I found that wanting to please "man" with a cute slim body was not the best motivation for me. I resented it. It did not work well.

  I have **_washed_** my mind and heart with a new motivation:

My motivation is to stay healthy for God, out of gratitude for all He has done in my life and who He is. I have a desire to be a strong healthy "vessel" or home for Him; the Holy Spirit. My other motivation is to stay healthy to share my testimony and the Good News. I want to stick around and enjoy time with my husband, family and friends too.

- *Food Habits:* I have slowly acquired habits that usually work for me. We heard that it takes 21 days to develop new habits and break an addiction. However, sugar is a tough one. For several years now I have been working on breaking the sugar addiction, knowing that *sugar feeds cancer.* My husband and I decided to keep our home free of most sweets, sodas and packaged foods high in carbohydrates or high fructose corn syrup. We buy foods such as organic vegetables, fruits, nuts, wild caught fish, eggs, cheese, avocados, olive oil and coconut oil, dark chocolate, free-range chicken and other healthy prepared dishes. I find it to be a worthwhile challenge to create healthy scrumptious food. It takes a bit more time for meal prep, but gets easier over time. It is worth the effort. My husband says, "We eat the *forgiving* Keto Diet."

Food Prayer:

*"God forgive me for over eating. Help me to do better today. Help me to buy and eat foods that are good for my body. Thank you for giving me this wonderful "temple" to take care of. Help me with my 'self control'. I am grateful for my body. Help me to love others **as** I love myself. In Jesus name, Amen."*

- *Exercise:* With exercise, I try to be fun and flexible. My goal is 30-60 minutes of some form of exercise 6 days a week. It can be a Pilates class, walk around the neighborhood, bike ride, swimming laps or an exercise video. Whenever I can walk or take the stairs, I do it. Again, the motivation is to be healthy for God. The trim body follows: **"Eat to Live, don't live to eat."**

- *The Ketogenic Lifestyle, is eating mostly healthy fats, protein and veggies.* Very little carbs, sugar and prepared foods.

Intermittent fasting and 3-day fasts done for spiritual reasons, often helps with physical health as well. Studies show that defective cells starve (die-off) during a fast.

Perfectionism:

Better done than perfect. This is the motto that has helped me become "un-paralyzed" from my perfectionism. I was raised in a family where we strove for perfection and high standards. While striving for excellence is valiant, striving for perfection is often harmful. Remember we are saved by God's Grace through Faith; ***not*** by being a "perfect person," or by doing "perfect works." Things are never perfect enough for the perfectionist. Often perfection driven people will avoid starting a job, project or activity because they fear it will not be done perfectly. The "inner critic" stops us from performing. Many people fear criticism from others, as well (did you notice I didn't indent this paragraph).

I am learning to ***laugh at myself*** when I make mistakes. It has taken fifty years to learn that skill. I am trying to go easier on myself and others. The book *Hope for the Perfectionist* helped me.

Many of us have a tendency to try and fix things. I am learning to ***let go*** and ***let God***. An advisor suggested being flexible and open to the way things turn out; okay with one of several outcomes.

My counselor always said, *"Elizabeth, the Savior already came, and it wasn't you!"* ☺

Remedies

My Favorite Natural Remedies and Supplements:

Over the years, I have spent hours researching health issues and natural remedies. It is important for everyone to do their own research, including talking to physicians or naturopath doctors. Pray for God's guidance on what will work best for you.

I am sharing with you what has helped me with healing and maintaining excellent health.

Depression and Anxiety:

Use prayer and *recite scriptures* that relate to anxiety and depression. Philippians 4:6-7 states: *"Do not be anxious about anything. But in everything, by prayer and petition, with thanksgiving, present your requests to God. And the peace of God, which transcends all understanding, will guard your hearts and minds in Christ Jesus."*

When we worry, we are showing a lack of trust in God, and too much trust in ourselves. We can ask God to forgive us, and ask God to help us trust Him more.

Repentance is not a popular word; however when we admit that we are *missing the mark*, then seek forgiveness and change our thoughts and behavior, there is freedom. When we live *in sin*, our conscience plagues us, but with God's help we become free from the destructive habit. My go-to verse on this is from 1 John 1:9, *"If we confess our sins, He is faithful and just to forgive us our sins and to cleanse us from all unrighteousness."*

A few more tips:

- **Exercise-** My husband notices that I am in a super good mood on the days I go to my exercise class....hmmmm.

- **Fish Oil supplement capsules** (one with a high EPA-700mg or so) I take 2-4 per day, and notice a huge difference in my attitude! Burp-less liquid soft gels are preferred. 'Buy one get one free' works for me).

- ***Avoid prescription drugs if possible!*** Most have detrimental side effects including depression, weight gain and constipation—which is all depressing in itself. I was particularly affected negatively by birth control pills, when I was younger, as I gained ten pounds. I also found Antidepressants caused me to sleep until noon! Most drugs have metal toxicity, like aluminum, which may cause Alzheimer's. One non-prescription remedy for depression, used widely in Europe is **St. John's Wort**. It works.

- **Less sugar**—sugar causes an initial "High" followed by a "Low"—hence the name, "Sugar Blues"— Eat less processed foods and more vegetables, salads, and fruit. I prefer treats made with honey, stevia, molasses or maple syrup rather than sugar.

- **Less alcohol** (or none at all) It is *a depressant—*

  Remember: *"The higher one gets at night, the lower one feels in the morning."*

- **Laughing** and talking with friends lifts the mood.

- **20-30 Minutes of sunshine per day** (no sunscreen and no midday sun), Vitamin D helps with depression and is a cancer fighter! Sunshine produces mood-lifting serotonin in the brain!

- Getting on the **same page** with my husband. Daily chats.

- **Christian counseling**. I have attended MANY counseling sessions over the years.

- **Singing songs of gratitude** and of God's love and mercy. Sing along to Christian radio or CDs.

- **Keep a Gratitude Journal.** List 3 things each day.

- **Have a daily constant attitude of Repentance and Gratitude.** "God, I am sorry for ...God thank you for..."

- **Walks in nature,** swimming, simplifying life, fellowship with other believers at church or Bible study or "Moms in Prayer group"- where we get together to pray for our children.

- **Getting out of debt!** Christian Author/lecturer Dave Ramsey has great classes and some free materials online.

- **Working through parenting issues,** try the "Love and Logic" series of books and CD's and free weekly online pointers. Visit: www.loveandlogic.com/parenting, website and click on "join" for **free** weekly pointers.

- **Forgiveness;** giving and receiving it.

A friend once told me, "You know you've completely forgiven someone when you feel more sorry for them than you do yourself." Wow! Think about that for a minute...

- Looking at challenges in life as *"opportunities."*

- I have created a ***Prayer Closet/War Room.*** Handing concerns to God.

- Helping the downtrodden; Soup-kitchens, mission trips or helping the homeless. Shifts the focus off of ourselves.

- **Being "OK" with one of several outcomes** for any given situation.

- **Pray and fast**—every time you get hungry stop and pray for a specific person or concern. This helps with anxiety because it is taking action regarding the concern.

- **The cheapest "face-lift" and "mood-lift" is a smile.**

- "Be still and know that I am God." Slow down. Simplify.

- **Ask ministers to pray over you.** (James 5:14)

- The *ultimate remedy* is to ask **God to forgive our sins, and make Jesus the Lord and leader of our life.** The goal is to turn from our bad habits and *stinking thinking.*

Cancer:

Ask Church Elders for prayer with **healing oil.** (James 5:14-16)
When Ye Pray, Believe!

- **Reduce sugar and carbohydrate** consumption and consider the Ketogenic lifestyle, Atkins, Whole 30 or. Sugar feeds cancer, and carbs turn into sugar once ingested. Google: **Starving Cancer: Ketogenic diet a Key to Recovery-CBN.**

- **Break the sugar addiction.** Pray for God's help. Cancer "Lights up" during a PET Scan when the body is injected with sugar-water (glucose). That is how they often check to see if cancer is present in the body. Sugar is cancer fertilizer.

- Read the book, ***Chris Beats Cancer,*** before starting any cancer treatments. His message is revolutionary!

- **Forgive everyone! Studies show that unforgiveness and bitterness** block the immune system from functioning properly. Ask God to help you with this difficult process.

- **Drink tons of green tea**—organic mostly decaf.

- **Exercise:** the oxygen that exercising stirs up in the blood kills cancer cells. So it is really pretty easy; *sugar feeds cancer and oxygen kills cancer.*

- **Get enough sleep** for body to repair (1 mg. melatonin).

- **Reduce or avoid alcohol.** There are literally hundreds of studies that link it to cancer. Do your own research.

- **Eat an organic** *salad* with every lunch and dinner.

- **Sweat** out toxins by exercise or dry saunas.

- **Vitamin C; in mega-doses 2000 to 8000 mg.** daily, **Vitamins E and Selenium, Vitamins D and K. CoQ 10. Curcumin, Ground flax seed, Garlic, Fish oil, Alfalfa, Ginger, B Vitamins, Folic Acid.**

- **Research "The Truth about Cancer."**

- **Cruciferous vegetables** are big antioxidants!

- **Juicing** or blender drinks with tons of organic veggies.

- **Studies** have shown that the following foods may reduce the risk of cancer, and even kill cancer cells:

  Broccoli, Carrots, Beans, Berries, Cinnamon, Nuts (walnut and brazil), Olive oil, Turmeric/Curcumin, Citrus, Ground Flaxseed, Tomatoes, Garlic, Fatty fish, Wild caught Salmon, Beets, Onion, Coconut oil, Flax Oil; Chia seeds and organic Turkey, Chicken, Pickles, Sauerkraut, Asparagus and Avocados.

- **Use** *BPA-Free* **plastic bottles.**

- **Avoid:** Microwaves, Birth Control Pills, Cell phone by ear, Diet or Sugary Sodas, Antiperspirant, Soy products.

- **Get rid of white stuff in kitchen—white rice, white pasta, white flour, white sugar, white bread, white milk.**

- **Eat organic!** The pesticides on non organics cause toxic build-up in the body. Look up the "Dirty Dozen."

- **Lemons** are thought to be: **"Natural Chemotherapy."** Research "Lemons fight cancer". Drink filtered or alkaline water with lemons. I even eat the rinds.

- **Prayer and fasting.** Doing a **three day fast** may rejuvenate cells in the immune system, starving the defective cells.

- Do what you are **"Called to do in life."** This brings peace. Ponder: *Why do you want to live?* God wants us to live an abundant life serving and glorifying Him.

- Give yourself a **lymph node massage.**

- Eat a *"Light breakfast"*, or even skip breakfast. Research Intermittent fasting (eat between noon and 7p.m. only).

- **Get alkalized!** Look up "Alkaline foods". Drink Alkaline, Purified, Mineral and Distilled Water.

- Eric makes us a drink every morning with **Bragg's Apple Cider Vinegar** (with the Mother), lemon, local honey, aloe vera juice (100%), Kambucha, and 1 teaspoon ground flaxseed. We call it my *natural chemotherapy*.

  BTW: *ground flaxseed is a miracle cleanser* for intestines- no more constipation!

- Eat lots of *garlic*, fresh cilantro and parsley. Detoxifies.

- **Frankincense** Oil--rub some on your body for healing. I rub it where the mastectomy scars are.

- **Castor oil compress** on the area where cancer is. It helps pull out toxins.(I pour some castor oil on a piece of flannel, place it on my gut or chest, cover with saran wrap then a heating pad for 1-2 hours.) Relieves stomach issues too.

- **Deep Breathing**--- Remember cancer hates oxygen.

- Organic beauty/ cleaning products (no parabens/toxins.)

- Get natural sunscreen. (with zinc oxide-)

- Use **Stainless steel pans.** Black, nonstick pans emit a toxic odor when heated.

- Use grape seed or coconut oil when cooking. Do not heat olive oil too hot when cooking, as it can turn carcinogenic.

- **Get 20-30 minutes of sun** every day for vitamin D.

- If you BBQ, make sure *not* to eat the charred black parts.

- Lunch meats with nitrites may cause cancer.

- Avoid "Round-up" spray in your yard. It is toxic.

God is our Great Physician, and we need to *follow the Holy Spirit guidance for our best path of health and healing.* Pay attention to your body and how you feel after certain foods or vitamins.

We remember the story of the woman who came to Jesus for healing. She spent *all* of her money on doctors, and "grew *not* better but worse". (Matthew 9:20-22, Mark 5:25-34, Luke 8: 43-44)

Also, in the Old Testament, King Asa had a serious foot disease. He did not seek the Lord's help; he relied only on his physicians (even after warnings), as a result, he died! (II Chronicles 16:12)

Sometimes we do need to seek medical help. God invented doctors too. We need to pray for guidance with any physical maladies. I am grateful to the doctors who helped me. I believe there are many good doctors. I believe they are trapped in a bad system. According to the book, *Chris Beat Cancer*, the revenue from cancer patients is $300,000 on average, and chemotherapy companies often give large commissions, or perks to private oncologists. Unfortunately, doctors have very little training in nutrition and natural remedies that heal.

I understand we are in partnership with God. He doesn't need our help to perform miracles, but He wants a relationship with us.

He wants us to repent of unhealthy behaviors, thoughts or idols. We can beg God to heal us, but if we are eating junk food and boozing 24/7, watching negative TV all day, or rely on doctors and drugs more than God, there may be consequences. I wonder if God is less inclined to perform miracles when we trust in doctors and pharmaceutical drugs more than Him?

One pastor wrote, 'By prayer and study of God's Word, I believe we are more inclined to hear and sense the promptings of the Holy Spirit. Then we can pray together with great authority and conviction, believing and receiving in God's good will for us.'

God's promises: "I will restore your health and heal your wounds" "by His stripes we are/were healed" and "Your faith has made your well".

Jesus said:

"If two of you agree about anything they ask, it will be done for them by my Father in heaven." (Matthew 18:19) The Holy Spirit often reveals what we can ask with confidence.

Ultimately, God is in control, He loves us and wants us healthy!

My current daily vitamin/supplement plan is below (give or take a couple capsules). Please do your own research:

- Multi vitamin.(Garden of Life)
- 2 fish oil capsules—with a high EPA—for mood elevation, and heart health.
- Vitamin D with Vitamin K.(Get tested for D occasionally-It is especially important to take in winter – sunshine pill!)
- CoQ10 for heart health and fighting cancer.
- Magnesium with Calcium 2/1 ratio (lowered my blood pressure).
- Vitamin C –mega-dose is an immune booster.
- Selenium with Vitamin E – a cancer fighter.
- Folic Acid -cancer fighter.

- Curcumin for reducing inflammation, fights cancer etc.
- Probiotic capsule for digestive health and *1mg.* of melatonin for sleep. Both at bedtime.
- Alfalfa capsules – eliminates toxins.
- Often, I add in Hair-Skin and Nails capsules, garlic, B 12, Multi Greens capsules, or organic green juice.

It helps to fast, and do an herbal laxative for cleansing. It is not wise to overdo vitamins, so space out ingesting them and rotate weekly/monthly. Many vitamins need to be taken with food.

I encourage you to do your own due diligence and pray about what supplements will help you.

We do budget finances for supplements. It is worth the cost to stay out of the expensive and painful hospital and doctor's office. I believe great health is a result of a combination of diet, exercise, supplements, prayer, faith, friends, family, hope, will to live, purpose, laughter, creativity, Christian counseling and Christian meditation. I encourage you to talk with a Natural Path Doctor and or Physician. If you are taking any Pharmaceutical medications, find out if they will work together with any supplements you want to take. Consider a natural route. I did.

Jesus said, "Daughter, your faith has healed you. Go in peace and be healed of your affliction." (Mark 5:34)

Sexual Libido and a healthy love life with your husband:

- During the day, ask your husband how you can help make his life easier (remember you **"get what you give"**). It helps to be **joyful and content** with the life they are working so hard to provide for us.

- **Work out a plan** with your husband for birth control and/or having children.

- Get **Christian counseling** to sort out any issues, so when you are in bed, you can focus on loving each other and not your problems.

- Keep the bedroom for sleep and lovin' only. We placed signs on the ceiling fan in our bedroom that said:

  "Bedroom is for sleeping, loving, reading and sweet talking...DO NOT discuss in-laws, ex's, money, or kids."

When either of us starts to talk about in-laws, ex's, kids or money, the other one turns on the ceiling fan, and the sign twirls and blows in the breeze! We try to talk about difficult issues on walks, in the kitchen, backyard or in Christian counseling.

- Set a **"date-night"** with your husband. Send him sweet texts during the day letting him know you are excited for the date! Put on some romantic—or salsa—music in your bedroom. A few other ideas to spice things up: some roses... put a few pedals on the bed. Dark chocolate.

- Use **Ylang Ylang** essential oil.

- **Romantic or fun lingerie**.

- A good *natural* gel lubricant is a must- Coconut Oil.

- **Ask** your husband what he would like in bed.

- **Focus on getting *closer*** to your husband and connecting with him through love making. Relax and enjoy.

God invented sex between a man and wife, and loves marriages that thrive in all areas: sexually, emotionally and spiritually. Pray that you and your spouse will always be super attracted to each other and enjoy a healthy sex life.

Recipes

Note: Use organic ingredients whenever possible for health and best flavor in all recipes:

Cabbage Soup

This recipe was told to me by my dental hygienist while she was cleaning my teeth. Jennifer, Kate and I made this delicious Cabbage Soup often as they were growing up. Have fun with this recipe…use whatever veggies you have in the fridge.

Ingredients:
½ head of cabbage chopped (or one bag of shredded cabbage)
1 yellow onion chopped
4-5 cloves garlic minced
1 red, yellow or green bell pepper chopped (or ½ of all 3!)
½ bunch of celery chopped
2 potatoes or carrots chopped small (or 1 of each)
2-3 cups of spinach chopped
1 large carton of Cream of Tomato~Red pepper Soup or 1 large bottle of V8 Juice.
1 large carton of organic vegetable or chicken broth
Salt and Pepper
½ bunch cilantro-chopped
Italian Herbs (1-2 T crushed between your fingers)
Few shakes of hot sauce
Big drizzle of olive oil
4 Bay leaves (optional)
4-6 organic, skinless, boneless chicken thighs (or 8 tenders) sautéed and chopped into pieces, or 2 cups of rotisserie chicken chunks (chicken optional)
Optional ingredients: ½ cup wild or brown rice, white beans, lentils, Italian parsley, barley, thyme, any other veggies.

Instructions: Sauté garlic and onion. Put all ingredients into a large pot. Cover with 2-3 cups of water and bring to a boil. Simmer for 40-60 minutes until done. Add extra water, salt and pepper as needed.

Top each bowl with a bit of grated cheese or a dollop of plain greek yogurt or avocado.

Serve with sprouted wheat toast or bagel.

I usually freeze a few Tupperware containers, or share with a neighbor.

Oh! We sometimes add 1 clean real stone to the soup to make it "Stone Soup." Whoever gets the stone at a pot-luck gets a prize!

Cozy dinner the fall or winter. ☺

Delicious Nutritious Banana Bread
My latest greatest version!

Ingredients:
½ cup olive oil or melted coconut oil (I use half of each)
½ cup honey (half maple syrup if you have it)
2 teaspoons vanilla extract
2 eggs
3 super ripe bananas mashed. Frozen bananas also work (just defrost, cut off end and squeeze out!) total of 1 cup.
1 teaspoon baking *soda*
½ teaspoon salt
2 cups organic *whole wheat white* flour (I often substitute ¼ cup oat bran, or ¼ cup ground flax seed)
¾ cup chopped pecans or walnuts (optional)
1 T Organic sugar for top.

Instructions:

1. Preheat oven to 325 degrees, grease 9 x 5 loaf pan.

2. Mix oil, honey, Maple syrup, vanilla, eggs, mashed bananas. Add baking soda and salt. Mix well.

3. Fold in flour until blended nicely, but don't over mix. (add a bit more flour if runny, or a splash of milk or water if too thick—batter should be thicker than cake batter) Fold in ½ cup nuts.

4. Pour batter into loaf pan. Sprinkle ¼ cup nuts on top and a tablespoon of sugar if you like. Bake about 55-65 minutes. Test with toothpick until it comes out clean (it often needs an extra few minutes).

Note: I usually double the recipe and make 1 loaf and 12 muffins. Muffins need just 20-ish minutes. After removing from oven I sometimes spread 2 tablespoon of butter on the top creating a glaze.

Keep loaf in the pan for 10 minutes then loosen edges with knife and put loaf out on rack or plate to cool. (Freezes well)

Serve plain, toasted, and with or without butter or honey. Yummy!

Fabulous Fish Tacos

It's a complete meal with all the food groups. Tasty and easy-ish!

Ingredients:
Small white corn tortillas- organic
3-4 fillets of Cod, Ahi or Mahi Mahi or salmon
1/2 Large red onion-chopped fine
1 Bunch cilantro, coarsely chopped
1 Bag of colorful shredded cabbage (or 2 cups chopped cabbage)
1 lime
1 clove garlic minced

Dressing- 4 tablespoons of organic mayonnaise or greek yogurt mixed with 2 tablespoons of any vinaigrette or Italian dressing and 1 tablespoon lime juice.
1-2 avocados cut in slices
1 Red bell pepper cut in slices

Instructions:

1. Toss cabbage with dressing and ¼ cup of cilantro and 2 tablespoons of onion and some minced garlic.

2. Cook fish with ¼ cup cilantro and rest of onion (on the side) in 2 tablespoons of coconut oil or olive oil for about 2-4 minutes per side (do not overcook-break open to test). Remove from pan and chop up fish. Squeeze on lime juice, salt and pepper. Cover to keep warm.

3. Fry tortillas in fry pan oil until light brown, flip and fold in half, making a shell. Place on paper towel.

4. Put fish mixture into each tortilla, top with cole-slaw mixture.

Garnish with red bell pepper slices and avocado and extra cole slaw on the side.

Serves 3-4

Veggie Wraps

My mom's recipe—try variations with veggies!

Ingredients:

2-4 spinach or wheat tortillas (Extra large)
4-6 Tablespoons herb cream cheese
1 ½ cups chopped fresh spinach
4 oz. sprouts (any kind)
2-4 slices of onion (I prefer purple, sliced super thin)
6-8 slices of tomato or red bell pepper
2-4 teaspoons chopped fresh basil
1 avocado sliced

2 Tablespoons vinaigrette
1 package organic chicken tenders- sautéed in olive oil and sliced into strips seasoned with salt and pepper. (Optional)

Instructions:
Lay out tortillas. Smear with cream cheese all the way to edges. About two inches from the bottom edge, add the rest of the ingredients in a horizontal line so that ½ of the tortilla is covered, drizzle with vinaigrette. Flip the two-inch portion of the tortilla over the filling and roll tightly. The cream cheese will act like glue and seal the tortilla. Cut in half, or in 1 inch pinwheels.

Serve and enjoy!

Serves 2- 4

Fiesta Frittata---9x13 glass pan- brunch or dinner

This crust less quiche recipe is a combination of recipes, from the "Cookie Lady" of Piedmont, Grandmother Logan's Zucchini casserole recipe, and Tahoma Meadows Basic Frittata.

Ingredients:
10 eggs
¼ cup milk (any kind)
1 T Italian herbs, salt and pepper, 1 T mustard.
2 tablespoons olive oil
5-6 cups of chopped veggies such as; red, yellow, green pepper, onions, spinach, asparagus, garlic, artichoke, olives, sundried tomatoes, mushrooms, garlic, zucchini, cilantro or basil.
Sauté veggies lightly in olive oil.
1-2 cups shredded cheese (any combination of jack, parmesan, and cheddar)
2-3 Organic sausages cooked and chopped (optional)

Garnish: Cilantro, avocado, plain greek yogurt, hot sauce.

Instructions:

Grease 9 x 13 pan

Layer on sautéed veggies (sausage)
Layer cheese on top of veggies

Wisk eggs, milk and seasonings in a bowl, and pour evenly over top.

Bake at 350 degrees until golden brown, and middle is set, not jiggly, approximately 45 minutes.

Serve with a green salad or fruit salad. Freezes well too!

Jennifer's Strawberry Green Salad

Ingredients:

Salad greens (any small bag of organic)
Sliced strawberries (a dozen or more, organic)
Cherry tomatoes (half a basket or more of organic)
¼ cup of pine nuts (or pecans chopped)
1 avocado- diced
Cheese--crumbled goat or blue (approx. 1/3 cup)
Dressing: any vinaigrette, or make your own with:
½ c olive oil, ¼ c balsamic or cider vinegar, 1 squirt Dijon mustard, black pepper, 3 crushed garlic cloves, 1 T of honey- Wisk together.

Instructions:

Toss salad with dressing and serve on plates.

To make this a complete meal, cook some salmon or albacore-tuna steaks in olive oil and butter for 3-5 minutes per side on medium heat, and place fish on the top of the salad, or on the side. Enjoy!

For more recipes, remedies and lessons, watch for Elizabeth's new book on "God's Food" due out in 2019.

Acknowledgments

Thanks to my amazing husband, Eric Soldahl for his unending encouragement, editing, and love. Thanks to Heather Bowers, Pastor Courtney, Debbie McMaster, Katie Monroe, Grayson Soldahl and Erica Prior for their thoughtful input and editing.

Thank you to my family and friends for their love and support: Mom and Dad~ Mary Ellen and Bob Logan, children: Jennifer, Kate, Grayson, Nolan, Amber and Paul. Brothers; Mark and Don. Mother-in-law Florence Soldahl, Robynn Coulter, Kimberly Woods, Jamelle Dewees, Karen Jones, Jerolyn Soldahl, Nancy and Steve Hertzog, Esther and Andy Hur, Dolores Heaton, Frida Paredes, Karen and Rich Eddy, Olivia Angeli, Sue Parkins, Keven Campbell, Mitch and Melody Forrester, Bob Bohling, Maria and Jesus Tafoya, Ian, Cathy, and Angie Naef, The Fullers, Margaret Fisher, Cindy Woodrum, Carol Johnson, Winnie Larson, Krissy Richardson, June Brooke, Tiffany Burson, Joyce Sears, Amanda Taylor, "Cassie," Judy Drake, Roger and Sandee Babcock, Christopher Melton, Noble and Sharleen Spees, Mark and Susan Collins, Mark and Marie Cook, Marion Knox, Grant and Ruth Henning, Danette Varga, Karen Morse, Dr. Godby, Dr. Ramos, Dr.Rathbun, Dr.Mentakis, Dr Davis, Dr. Claudia DeYoung.

Elizabeth's Recommended Reading list

1. New Spirit Filled Life Bible; KJV, New King James Version.
2. The Excellent Wife, Martha Peace ~ my go-to book for any issues in my marriage.
3. Chris Beat Cancer: A comprehensive Plan for Healing Naturally, Chris Wark
4. Love and Logic Parenting, (all books), Cline & Fay
5. Boundaries, Townsend and Cloud ~ all Boundary Books.
6. The Hiding Place, Corrie Ten Boom
7. Safely Home, Randy Alcorn
8. The Enneagram made Easy- 9 Personality Types- Wagele
9. Hope for the Perfectionist, Dr. David Stoop
10. The Trouble with Truth, *Balancing Truth & Grace*, Renfroe
11. Simplify Your Life, Elaine St. James
12. The Road Less Travelled, Scott Peck
13. People of the Lie, Scott Peck
14. Grace for Each Hour, Mary Nelson ~on breast cancer.
15. Precious Bible Promises
16. The Little Bible
17. Lucy Libido, There's an Oil for That ~ essential oils.
18. Bragg Healthy Lifestyle, Bragg & Bragg
19. God's Way to Ultimate Health, Malkmus & Dye
20. Becoming a Contagious Christian, Mittelberg, Strobel
21. From Hero to Zero and Redeemed, Eric Soldahl
22. Spiritual Firepower - Unleashed! Eric Soldahl
23. Speaking the Truth in Love, Koch & Haugk
24. Facing the Facts, Jones~God's design for sex (for teens.)
25. Codependent No More, Melody Beatie
26. Surviving the Prodigal Years, Marcia Mitchell

Support Groups:

1. Celebrate Recovery (Christ centered recovery group for addictions/habits), Alcoholics Victorious, Overcomers Outreach.
2. Moms in Prayer
3. Hearts Being Healed Conferences
4. Stephen Ministry
5. Bible Study Fellowship
6. Christian Counseling

DVDs and CDs and TV shows:

1. The 700 Club~ on TBN/CBN(Christian Broadcast Network)
2. Greg Laurie—Harvest Ministries
3. Marcus & Joni
4. Boundaries, Townsend and Cloud
5. Financial Peace, Dave Ramsey
6. Battlefield of the Mind, Joyce Meyer
7. Love and Logic (all in series)~Fay & Cline
8. The Truth Project Series
9. War Room
10. Fireproof
11. Mother Theresa~ Hennessey
12. Martin Luther~ Fiennes
13. Sound of Music~Julie Andrews
14. The Nativity story
15. "Jesus" film in over 1,500 languages
16. Tell Someone (Free online series)~Greg Laurie
17. Healing Praise CD~

More about Elizabeth

By the grace of God, Elizabeth is healthy and thriving. She and her husband Eric are Musical Missionaries spending their time sharing the Good News of Jesus' love, healing, forgiveness, and promise of everlasting life. They travel giving testimony and music at concerts, conferences, and various churches. They enjoy time with friends and family in the Lake Tahoe area, Santa Barbara, La Quinta, North and South Carolina, and the San Francisco Bay area. Elizabeth and Eric enjoy keeping up with their five children; all responsible young adults. Elizabeth leads a Pilates Health and Exercise class, continuing with her daily centering prayer time, Bible studies, Moms in Prayer group, singing, gardening, creative Keto cooking, craft projects, walking, and remodeling projects. Her greatest desire is to spread the John 3:16 and 2 Peter 3:9, Gospel message daily.

For more information on Elizabeth and Eric's Musical Missionary Ministry go to: www.Faithonfire.net

If Elizabeth's story was meaningful to you, please consider posting a review on Amazon.com*Direct link:* http://www.amazon.com/dp/173202460X

Made in the USA
Columbia, SC
13 March 2019